Fall Down, Stand Up

Fall Down, Stand Up

Advice for Aspiring Principals

Second Edition

Russ Thompson

ROWMAN & LITTLEFIELD
Lanham • Boulder • New York • London

Published by Rowman & Littlefield
A wholly owned subsidiary of The Rowman & Littlefield Publishing Group, Inc.
4501 Forbes Boulevard, Suite 200, Lanham, Maryland 20706
www.rowman.com

Unit A, Whitacre Mews, 26-34 Stannary Street, London SE11 4AB

Copyright © 2016 by Russ Thompson

All rights reserved. No part of this book may be reproduced in any form or by any electronic or mechanical means, including information storage and retrieval systems, without written permission from the publisher, except by a reviewer who may quote passages in a review.

British Library Cataloguing in Publication Information Available

Library of Congress Cataloging-in-Publication Data

Names: Thompson, Russ, 1955– author.
Title: Fall down, stand up : advice for aspiring principals / Russ Thompson.
Description: Lanham : Rowman & Littlefield [2015] | Includes bibliographical references and index.
Identifiers: LCCN 2015044204 (print) | LCCN 2016002381 (ebook) |
  ISBN 9781475826623 (cloth : alk. paper) | ISBN 9781475826630 (pbk. : alk. paper) |
  ISBN 9781475826647 (Electronic)
Subjects: LCSH: School principals—Vocational guidance—United States. |
  School principals—Professional relationships—United States.
Classification: LCC LB2831.92 .T45 2015 (print) | LCC LB2831.92 (ebook) |
  DDC 371.2/012—dc23
LC record available at http://lccn.loc.gov/2015044204

∞™ The paper used in this publication meets the minimum requirements of American National Standard for Information Sciences—Permanence of Paper for Printed Library Materials, ANSI/NISO Z39.48-1992.

Printed in the United States of America

*To my wife, Betty-Jean, for her
constant love and support.*

Contents

Foreword		xi
Preface		xv
Acknowledgments		xix

DISCIPLINE — 1

1	The Problem Was Now Worse	3
2	Class Time Was Like Lunch Time	5
3	It Was the Best He Had Seen	7
4	Simple Detention	11
5	He Had to Change His Mentality	15
6	Saturday School	19
7	Lunch Supervision	23
8	A Fight That Was Prevented	25
9	The Problem with Suspensions	29
10	The First Award of His Entire Life	31
11	It Was Almost a Real Emergency	33
12	Riot and Recovery	35
13	Section Review	39

CLASSROOM INSTRUCTION — 41

| 14 | The Learning in Classrooms | 43 |

15	The Reason It Worked	47
16	A Sustained Process	51
17	He Had Firmly Believed	55
18	You Have to Go Out and Look for Problems	57
19	The Best Way to Spend Your Time	59
20	It Was His First Day	61
21	An Opinion Is Not Research	63
22	Your Presence in Classrooms	65
23	Will It Help Students Learn Better?	67
24	The Power of a Positive Learning Environment	69
25	The Common Core State Standards	71
26	A Model Lesson	83
27	Section Review	85

SCHOOL OPERATIONS — 87

28	Cleaning Needed	89
29	The Foundation of Your Entire School	91
30	Tragedy	93
31	Another Tragedy	95
32	Almost a Disaster	99
33	Phone Calls	101
34	The Entire Contract	103
35	The Right Kind of Faculty Meeting	105
36	Section Review	107

LEADERSHIP — 109

37	Delegation	111
38	Delegation Gone Bad	113
39	Deadlines	115
40	Ask Questions	117
41	A Sacrifice You Must Make	119

42	Priorities	121
43	Also Listen to the Quiet Voices	123
44	We Are Not As Bad As . . .	125
45	Making People Happy Is Not Your Job	127
46	He Went Over to His Shelf	129
47	Pick Up the Phone	133
48	A Leader Who Got Things Done	135
49	Do Not Let the Obstacle Overcome You	137
50	Exhaustion	139
51	A Mistake He Would Never Forget	141
52	Advice from a Pro	143
53	Target Practice	145
54	Ask for Advice	147
55	A Big Difference	149
56	Always Watching You	151
57	Section Review	153

PEOPLE — **155**

58	In the Middle of Kids	157
59	It Was Distorted and Very Negative	159
60	People Need Time	161
61	Suggestion or Requirement?	163
62	Saved by a Recording Device	165
63	Necessary Action	167
64	It Was Said Behind His Back	169
65	It Was a Lie and the Principal Believed Him	171
66	Gossip	173
67	Delay Makes It Worse	175
68	Talk to the Person in Person	177
69	You Must Also Be Persuasive	179

70	Remember the Positives	181
71	A Good School Again	183
72	Section Review	185

| Index | 187 |
| About the Author | 189 |

Foreword

If you are looking for a grand, sweeping theory of leadership, don't buy this book.

If you are looking for practical, tested knowledge, and strategies for leading large and challenging schools, buy it.

Buy two copies if you are a leader in a troubled secondary school.

You can trust the wisdom and knowledge this book provides, because Russ Thompson has the credentials to be credible, and the honesty to be candid. For thirty-six years, he was a teacher, mentor, dean, assistant principal, and principal at secondary schools in southern California. During fourteen of his thirty-six years, he was a principal of large, diverse high schools. He also served as a director of high school services, responsible for supporting and developing school principals. He served during a time of major challenges—economic downturns and school cutbacks, multiple reform movements, and turbulent political controversies. He saw it all, prospered, and wrote a book that shares what he learned.

But Russ is not offering tricks. Tricks won't help you. Legendary basketball coach John Wooden of UCLA taught this piece of wisdom: "If you keep too busy learning the tricks of the trade, you may not learn the trade" (Wooden, 1997, p. 93).

Russ offers solid ideas and strategies for dealing with the dozens of problems and dilemmas that confront a school principal. You can solve problems; but dilemmas, you can only manage, not solve, because they are par for the course in schools.

In the section on discipline, Russ establishes that it is an inevitable dilemma arising from assembling in one place immature youngsters of varying backgrounds and temperaments. If you don't want to learn how to manage the behavior problems that arise every day, you'd better find an alternative to being a principal. Discipline is not something you do when a problem arises. Russ provides rich, compelling examples of another approach: create a school discipline system which prevents as many behavior problems as possible, and have in place responses when they do arise. But don't make it something that only the principal owns. The discipline system has to be owned by everyone: faculty, staff, students, and parents. When something happens, be sure that everyone knows how to respond, and what will happen as a consequence. Fighting, race-related riots, tardiness, and defiant behavior, among other problems, are discussed chapter by chapter. Practical, workable solutions are offered with examples drawn from Russ's long career—examples that will be instantly recognizable to anyone who has worked in a modern public school.

Some might ask why the section on classroom instruction comes after discipline. Well, Russ knows that before teaching and learning can begin, the student has to be ready, able, and willing. It is true that the best way to deal with behavior problems is to have students studying history and mathematics. But for the principal dealing with the dilemmas and problems of discipline, it is critical to have a school-wide system in place and bought into by everyone. It is just as important as the teacher making clear on day one of a new year what the rules of her classroom will be. Psychological research has demonstrated that all persons—youth and adult alike—are more likely to prosper when expectations are set, clear, and shared.

Given Russ's sensible approach to discipline, no informed educator will be surprised to learn that he starts the section on classroom instruction by emphasizing the role of principal as instructional leader. This is his rule: "Instructional leadership means keeping yourself focused on classrooms and instruction. How do you do that? First, you have to schedule your time to make sure that you and your administrators get into classrooms to observe for at least one hour every day. You must also spend the time that is necessary to meet with teachers and provide feedback."

Delegating instructional leadership to assistants and others is necessary in a large school with many faculty. But if the principal is not an active leader or is not engaged in identifying and supporting better teaching, then inevitably the improvement of instruction becomes a secondary priority. The principal has to lead by example—the whole point of schools is to create situations in which instruction is provided. Schools are not supported by tax dollars for discipline, efficient business operations, and well-run lunchrooms; these are conditions necessary to provide instruction and nurture learning.

Russ offers in the chapters of the learning section practical, instructional leadership strategies and tactics tied together by this piece of wisdom: "Your top priority must be classroom instruction, and you should be in classrooms constantly. Don't fall into a pattern where you are only visiting classrooms at certain times of the day. And keep a list to make sure you are getting into all of the classrooms. . . . If you cannot do anything else, make sure that you get into classrooms. It is a powerful way to provide leadership. The benefits are almost immeasurable. First, getting into classrooms helps you to find out what is happening instructionally. This gives you a true picture of the teaching that students are experiencing every day. Your observations will help you to determine the improvements that are most needed. Next, teachers feel supported when you get into their classrooms. It shows that you care about their efforts. And they will respect your feedback."

The section on school operations deals with the realities of schools. Facilities maintenance, scheduling, crisis management, student deaths, gang activity, union contracts, leader communication, and faculty meetings are among the issues addressed and discussed. This section is capped off with six pieces of golden wisdom for managing school operations:

1. Make sure that you have the strongest possible master schedule. Be sure that classes are balanced ahead of time and that every student is scheduled properly.
2. Provide teachers with the textbooks, instructional materials, and equipment they need.
3. Make sure that you have clean and well-maintained classrooms, buildings, and landscaping.
4. Read your teachers' contract and know it thoroughly.
5. Make sure that you scrutinize field trips very carefully.
6. Have plans in place for special needs, such as grief counseling and gang prevention.

In the section on leadership, Russ shares hard-won ideas and wisdom that can benefit any principal, especially those working in challenging schools. Any summary I can offer here would shortchange a rich library of practical knowledge. Instead, I urge anyone who is a principal or aspires to be one to have this book at hand. What Russ learned about leadership in his 36 years will make it a "turn to" resource.

The final section of the book deals with people—and all the good and not so good that can arise when human beings work together and associate over time. Although none of the illustrative examples indicate they were drawn from personal experiences, their authentic and believable quality suggests they were. Duplicity, manipulation, negativity, and gossip are things that people are capable of— this is unfortunate but so true. To be angered and frustrated by such aspects of human nature does little good, though no one skates untouched past the troubling behavior of adults who are working in professional roles. Russ urges we remember that the better angels of our nature are there in abundance in many schools and educators. As hard as it is to keep that in mind when trouble with people comes, he urges that principals respond by staying the course, staying close and listening to others, talking to students, teachers, and supervisors, and remembering the positives. Don't let the negatives that inevitably come obscure the positives.

Finally, there is an implicit ethic and fundamental principle that threads through this volume—one that reflects another of the aphorisms for which Coach John Wooden was famous: "When you improve a little each day, eventually big things occur . . . Not tomorrow, not the next day, but eventually a big gain is made. Don't look for the big, quick improvement. Seek the small improvement one day at a time. That's the only way it happens—and when it happens, it lasts" (Nater & Gallimore, 2010, p. 52).

Russ Thompson learned through his many years as an educator that the steady, relentless pursuit of better schooling and teaching is the thing that makes a principal effective and proud.

Ronald Gallimore, Ph.D.
Distinguished Professor Emeritus
University of California, Los Angeles

REFERENCES

Nater, S. & Gallimore, R. (2010). *You haven't Taught Until They have Learned: John Wooden's Teaching Principles and Practices*. Morganstown, West Virginia: Fitness International Technology, Inc.

Wooden, J. R. (with Steve Jamison). (1997). *Wooden: A Lifetime of Observations and Reflections On and Off the Court*. Lincolnwood (Chicago), IL: Contemporary Books.

Preface

It was a Friday night in October. There was a big crowd for homecoming, and the principal did not want to take any chances. He walked up the stairs to the top of the bleachers and spoke briefly with the two safety officers. The top row of the bleachers was sectioned off with yellow caution tape. This made it possible for the officers to observe the crowd from behind and move easily from side to side.

The principal looked down at the crowd. This was the section where most of the students sat. If there was going to be a problem, it would be here. The principal did not sense any tensions or see anybody who appeared to be gang related. He was hoping for a calm game with no incidents.

As the principal looked down, he noticed a middle-aged couple climbing up the steps toward him. The man was walking in front. The woman was walking behind him and holding his hand. It seemed unusual to the principal that the adults would want to sit in the student section.

When the couple reached the top, the man was smiling. "Do you remember me?" he said to the principal.

The principal looked at him closely. He saw a man in his mid-forties, with a few wrinkles and some flecks of gray in his hair. Then he recognized the smile and the look in his eyes.

"Robert!" said the principal. "I still remember you from seventh-grade English! It has been thirty years!"

They shook hands and embraced.

"I would like to introduce you to my girlfriend," said Robert. "This is Olivia. She used to go to school here."

"Olivia, I am so glad to meet you!" said the principal. "Robert was such a good writer. He was always such a positive influence on the rest of the class."

The principal paused and turned to Robert. "So what are you doing now?" said the principal.

"I am the vice president of a financial services company," said Robert. "We help people with their investments. I have been there for fifteen years."

"It doesn't surprise me," said the principal. "You were such a hard worker. You seem very happy."

"It is so great to see you," said Robert. "I still can't believe that you recognized me after all these years."

"You still have the same smile and the same look in your eyes," said the principal. "You always had such a positive outlook."

They continued talking for about ten minutes. The principal felt so happy to know that his former student was now successful.

* * *

What do students need to become successful? They need teachers who believe in them and care about them as people. They need teachers who are skilled and persistent in teaching them. They also need principals who are skilled and persistent in supporting their teachers.

When you do your job well as a principal, you are helping kids learn and become successful. It's about being out on your campus constantly, frequently getting into classrooms, and meeting with teachers to provide feedback. It's about talking with people to get their ideas and working with them to find the right answers. It's about being a good role model, both to students and teachers. It's about constantly trying to get better.

Starting out as a principal is a lot like starting out as a new teacher. You feel alone. You need guidance. And you must provide leadership even when you are not sure of yourself.

Continuing as a principal is just as hard. You get tired. You get frustrated. And the demands never stop. You are constantly facing new challenges, you are constantly in the spotlight, and you must constantly find ways to improve.

You must be determined and never back down, even when it seems like you are not making any progress. You must be patient with others and keep working with them, even when you become frustrated. You must be confident in your beliefs and persistent, even when it feels like you are all alone.

Serving as a principal is not easy. When you hit obstacles, you have to overcome them. When you make mistakes, you have to improve and keep trying. The pace is fast, the hours are long, and the challenges keep coming.

But there is nothing more rewarding than seeing a school improve. And there is no better feeling than going into a classroom and knowing that the students are learning at high levels. As a principal, more than anybody else, you get to have a direct effect on the teaching in every classroom and the success of every student.

There are times when you will stumble and get discouraged. But don't let that stop you. Remember your successes, remember your skills, and keep trying. Keep going and keep doing your best. Do not let the obstacles overcome you. Make up your mind that you will overcome the obstacles.

It is always better if you can learn from somebody else's mistakes. The stories in this book are real. In many cases, they describe errors and significant setbacks. I hope you will learn from the stories in this book, move forward, and work to create a school where every student learns at the highest levels every day.

Russ Thompson, Ed.D.

Acknowledgments

First, I am grateful to my wife, Betty-Jean. She sacrificed, supported, and encouraged me throughout my years as an educator. No matter what was happening in my career, she was always behind me. I am also grateful to our children, Genevieve, Nolan, Shannon, and Allison.

I would like to thank Dr. Stuart Bernstein, Frank Dolce, Dr. Julian Lopez, and Merle Price for giving me valuable feedback on the content of this book. I am grateful to our daughter, Shannon, for her assistance in editing. I would like to go back many years to thank one of my professors from Whitworth College (now Whitworth University), Dr. Tammy Reid, for believing in me as a writer.

I would also like to express my gratitude to all of the educators who have helped and guided me throughout my entire career. I am especially grateful to Dan Isaacs, Dr. Julian Lopez, and Dr. George McKenna. I will never forget what they taught me about leadership, mental toughness, striving for excellence, and never giving up.

DISCIPLINE

Chapter 1

The Problem Was Now Worse

It was a Thursday in February. The semester had started three weeks earlier. It was the fourth period, and the principal was walking east in front of the F Building.

There was a radio call from the main office. "415 in room D-12!"

The principal started running. There was a fight.

A campus supervisor was standing outside when the principal arrived at the classroom. A student in a gray hoodie was standing next to him. The student's nose was bleeding.

The principal went inside the classroom. Several students were out of their seats. Books and papers had been thrown all over. Some chairs in the middle of the room had been knocked over.

The teacher was at the side of the classroom, holding the arm of a student named Bobby. Bobby's shirt was dirty and bloody. His collar was also torn. The principal knew Bobby from previous incidents.

"What happened?" the principal asked the teacher.

"All of the kids were working," said the teacher. "Then Bobby got up and socked Leon in the face. It was a full-on fight."

The teacher had been there for three weeks. He was brand new, just out of college. When the principal had observed the teacher during the first week of the semester, he had seen serious discipline problems. The students were talking and having side conversations. They were eating and throwing food wrappers on the floor. They were also texting on their cell phones and listening to music.

The principal had met with the teacher prior to his assignment and provided materials on classroom discipline. He had also assigned an instructional coach to work closely with the teacher. But the problem was now worse. The principal knew that he had to act fast.

* * *

The lack of classroom discipline is a critical problem that destroys learning and causes many good people to leave the teaching profession. It seriously hurts students by creating constant distractions that make it impossible for them to concentrate on learning. It destroys teachers by causing constant frustration and making it impossible for them to concentrate on teaching.

One disruptive student can ruin learning for every student in an entire classroom. If you do not have a school environment where adults are in control, you cannot improve learning.

Are teachers going to come to you and ask for help if they are experiencing discipline problems? In many cases, they will not. They might not understand the seriousness of the problem. They may worry about getting a negative evaluation. They might also be embarrassed.

So what do these teachers do? Many of them cope with their frustrations and develop negative attitudes about kids. Some of them develop methods of controlling kids that are negative and hurtful. Many of them come to believe that students don't want to learn. It's like a disease that can spread from teacher to teacher and bring down an entire school.

If your school is having discipline problems, you can solve them if you face up to the situation with the determination to prevail. You must make it your goal that every adult will get full cooperation from every student. You must strive to create a learning environment where every teacher in your school can focus on teaching, not on maintaining discipline.

Improving discipline is about much more than raising academic achievement and creating an orderly school environment. It's about helping students grow and learn the rules that will help them become successful in life. Students who break the rules of school will often become the adults who break the rules of society. This hurts everybody.

By correcting negative behaviors early and showing students how to make positive choices, you are not just helping students improve academically. You are helping them become better people. You are providing them with the skills that will help them to achieve success wherever they go in life.

Chapter 2

Class Time Was Like Lunch Time

It was the middle of second period, during the first week in October. The principal was talking with the sheriff's deputy assigned to the school. They were sitting on a bench in Senior Square. The campus was deserted.

"Last year there would have been two hundred kids wandering around here during second period," said the deputy. "Class time was like lunch time."

The principal looked around at the empty campus. "This is what happens when you have the right set of rules and consequences. The kids who were ditching class last year are now attending class this year."

* * *

The school had been out of control for several years. Students would wander around the campus without going to class. Drug use, fights, and gang activity occurred regularly.

Racial conflicts sometimes exploded into riots, with police on campus and helicopters overhead. During one of the riots, students forced their way into a home economics classroom and pushed past the teacher to steal knives out of the kitchen drawers.

Teachers could not teach and students could not learn. It had been so bad for so long that nobody thought it could get better.

The school improved through the establishment of effective discipline. First, you must establish a clear set of rules. Second, you must create consequences that are reasonable, fair, and escape-proof. Third, your staff must work as a team to ensure the rules are enforced consistently.

You need administrators, counselors, and deans who are skilled in working with students and their parents. You need strong supervision in all areas of your campus. You must also provide rewards to encourage students who are doing a good job.

Chapter 3

It Was the Best He Had Seen

The principal was meeting with an administrator from the school district and two consultants. They had just spent more than an hour walking through the campus and going into all of the buildings. The objective of the tour was to identify areas of the school where architectural changes could be made to create small learning communities.

When the meeting was almost over, the administrator had one last thing to say. "I have visited almost fifty high schools," he said. "I would like to compliment you on the condition of your campus."

"Thanks," said the principal. "We have a great plant manager and a great custodial crew."

"The campus is very clean," said the administrator. "But I don't mean the cleanliness of the campus. It's about the kids. When the bell rang, all of the students were in class. And there were no students out of class during class time. This is the most orderly high school campus I have ever seen."

* * *

By taking the right steps to improve student conduct, you can create a positive leaving environment that benefits everybody. With a calm learning atmosphere that is free of disruptions, teachers can enjoy their work and focus on providing lessons that are interesting and engaging. Students can focus on learning at high levels to prepare themselves for college. Academic achievement rises, and everybody wins.

The first step in improving discipline is to meet with everybody involved to find out what is happening and ask for suggestions. These meetings should include administrators, teachers, parents, students, and support staff.

A good technique when you conduct these meetings is to record comments on chart paper or on a computer connected to an LCD projector. This makes the meetings go quicker, because people don't feel that they need to repeat themselves when they see that their comments are being written down. It also provides you with a permanent record that will help you with planning.

The most important task is to listen carefully and place a high value on everything said. This work will become the foundation for your improvement plan.

The next step is to draft a simple system of rules and consequences to improve student conduct. When you develop this plan, it is important to remember that the more you control minor problems such as tardiness, the more you will prevent big problems such as gang activity.

This is similar to the "broken window" strategies implemented by William Bratton when he was the police commissioner in New York City. By ensuring that small violations are fully addressed, major problems will decrease dramatically.

The rules and consequences that you draft should then be shared with staff members, parents, and students. When you have completed the process of getting feedback, you should then develop your final plan. Once the final plan has been developed, you should communicate it thoroughly through faculty meetings, letters to parents, and student assemblies.

If students are not getting to class on time, tardy sweeps should be a big part of your plan. These should be implemented every day, every period. Administrators, deans, counselors, and campus supervisors should be stationed throughout all areas of your campus during all passing periods.

When the tardy bell finishes ringing, any students who are out of class should report to a central location where their names will be recorded and they will be assigned a consequence such as detention.

Lengthening the duration of your bells to ten or twelve seconds will make this policy easier to implement, because students who are running late will have time to rush to class and get inside before the tardy bell finishes ringing.

A detention program is needed so that teachers have a meaningful consequence to assign for classroom misbehavior. An effective detention program must be escape-proof and excuse-proof.

A good way to achieve this is to assign students to serve detention in a designated detention room during lunch. If students cannot serve detention during lunch, they write a two-page essay at home explaining how to be successful in school. Teachers who assign detention should be required to call home and discuss the problem with a parent.

If students do not complete their detention or complete their essay by the following school day, the teacher sends the student to the dean, and the student gets a stronger consequence.

Students are smart. When you have a simple and fair set of rules and consequences that you always enforce, they will conduct themselves at very high levels. This will enable you to build a positive school culture where teachers can focus on teaching and students can concentrate on learning.

Chapter 4

Simple Detention

It was a Tuesday afternoon and lunch was almost over. There had been a pep rally for the basketball team on the outdoor stage. The band and drill team had also performed.

At 1:10 p.m., the bell rang and lunch was over. Fifteen-hundred students started walking to class.

The principal was standing on the quad, watching the students carefully. He was also watching his watch. At 1:13 p.m., he made the first call. "Three minutes!" he called out. "You have three minutes!" The other staff members were also echoing the call.

At 1:14 p.m., the principal was standing near the D Building. "Two minutes!" he called out. The campus started to clear. Most of the teachers were standing outside their doorways as the students entered their classrooms.

"Ninety seconds!" called the principal. Some students on the other side of the quad started running.

"One minute!" called the principal. More students were now running.

"Thirty seconds!" called the principal. The campus was almost empty.

"Fifteen seconds!" called the principal. Three students were still out of class in the D row.

At 1:16 p.m., the bell rang and the D row was clear. All of the students had made it to their classes on time.

The supervision staff began sweeping the campus. When the principal stopped by the deans' office, he noticed that five students had been tardy. Their names were being entered into the computer for detention. Their parents would also be called. The students would then be sent to class.

* * *

Controlling tardiness is essential in the effort to improve school-wide discipline and create a positive learning environment. If students understand that they must be on time, they will also understand that they must follow the other rules.

An effective way to reduce tardiness is to create a guidance room with deans where you send all students who are tardy. When students get to the guidance room, you assign them to serve a twenty-minute detention if they are tardy during period one. If they are tardy during periods two through six, you assign them to serve three detentions.

By sending students to the guidance room, you ensure that all students who are tardy will receive detention. Without this consistency, many students will continue to be tardy.

Accurate record keeping for detentions is also essential. You also need a simple way for numerous people to gain access to the records. By using Google Sheets, the spreadsheet program on Google Drive, you can make it possible for numerous people to view and update detention records.

If a student is tardy, enter a "T" next to the name. If a student is disobedient, enter a "D" next to the name. When the detention has been served, simply delete the letter.

An effective way for students to serve detention is have them report to a central location during lunch. This is important for safety, because it allows students to walk home after school in their normal groups and not alone. Having detention during lunch also prevents conflicts with after-school activities.

When students serve detention, they complete a one-page essay (front side, letter-size paper) explaining how to be successful in school. If they finish before their twenty minutes are up, they get to leave early, which gives them enough time to get their food and eat. It is also a good idea to let students eat, if they wish, while they are serving detention.

It is essential to have a system to ensure that students serve detention. As much as possible, parents should be called when students are assigned to serve detention. This is a proactive measure that also reinforces the punishment value.

It is also very important to have a backup system in case phone calls do not work. If students fail to report on their own to serve detention, set up a system to pick them up before lunch and walk them to the detention location. As an additional consequence, assign them to write a two-page essay (front and back, legal-size paper) instead of a one-page essay on letter-size paper.

It is also very important to allow teachers to assign detention for classroom infractions. An effective method for doing this is to provide a special mailbox where teachers submit detention slips. A staff member then enters the detention slips into Google Sheets.

This is a simple system that provides consistent, escape-proof detention if students violate school or classroom rules. This brings about significant improvements in student conduct, because students receive fair and consistent consequences if they break the rules.

Chapter 5

He Had to Change His Mentality

It was after school on the Monday of the fourth week of February. The principal was meeting with the new teacher from room D-12. There had been a fight in the teacher's classroom on the previous Thursday. The students would not listen to anything the teacher said, and his classes were out of control. An assistant principal and an instructional coach were also at the meeting.

"So how do you feel about things?" the principal asked.

"I knew it would be hard," said the teacher. "But I didn't think it would be this hard. To tell you the truth, I am seriously thinking about quitting teaching."

"You came into a very tough situation," said the principal. "Your classes had five long-term substitutes during the first semester. None of the teachers were able to establish themselves."

"So what should I do?" the teacher asked.

"A similar thing happened to me when I started teaching," said the principal. "My classes were noisy and the kids would not pay any attention to me. The students would throw things at me when I turned my back to write on the chalkboard. The only way I could get the students to be quiet was to give them busywork."

"So what did you do?" the teacher asked.

"I finally reached a turning point," said the principal. "One day I was sitting at my desk trying to help a girl with a writing assignment. Most of the other students were noisy and playing around. The girl could tell by the look on my face that I just wasn't making it. Then she asked me if I was going to quit too."

"So what did you do?" the teacher asked.

"I stood up and started yelling at the students to be quiet," said the principal. "I had to yell several times. Finally they got quiet and started working."

"What happened after that?" the teacher asked.

"I was very lucky," said the principal. "There were some teachers at the school who really took me under their wing and helped me. They told me that I had to be strict. They said that I was not helping the students by letting them take advantage of me. I started listening to those teachers, and it worked."

"Being strict did not come naturally to me," said the principal. "I had to change my mentality and teach myself how to be strict. I set up rules. I set up consequences for breaking the rules. I spent a lot of time calling parents. I used to write notes to myself on my lesson plans to be strict. Eventually I got to the point where discipline was no longer an issue for me. I was able to focus on teaching, not discipline."

* * *

This was a new teacher who was having very little success with his students. He was unable to teach because of constant disruptions. He was very frustrated, and he was considering leaving the teaching profession. The students were unable to learn.

By the end of the school year, he was a much stronger teacher who had very few discipline problems. He was able to enjoy teaching and focus on the learning needs of his students. The following discipline plan made it possible for him to turn things around:

SUGGESTED DISCIPLINE PLAN FOR CLASSROOM TEACHERS

Nothing should happen in your classroom unless it brings about learning and you want it to happen. You must communicate your expectations very clearly and have an assertive, take-charge attitude. If students misbehave, you must be firm and fully consistent in following through with consequences. You will not gain the respect of your students if you are inconsistent or depend upon others to enforce your rules for you. The discipline must come from you. You must also call home to gain the assistance of parents.

Class Rules

1. Bring all supplies.
2. Be seated and ready to work before the tardy bell rings.
3. Raise your hand and get permission to speak or leave your seat.
4. No food, gum, candy, or electronic devices.
5. Show respect at all times.

Consequences

1. You will get one warning for breaking any classroom rule.
2. Three warnings in the same week will cause twenty minutes of detention.
3. You will serve detention by reporting to the multi-purpose room during lunch. Your parents will also be called.
4. Repeated violations will cause a referral to the dean's office.

How to Use This Plan

1. Adapt the above rules and consequences to fit your own teaching style. Copy the rules onto posters in big letters that students can read from their seats. Teach the program to your students in the same way you would teach a normal lesson.
2. When giving a warning or a consequence, do so in a calm manner. Make a record on a roll sheet or clipboard so that students know you are serious about following through. Be sure to call home.
3. Make a seating chart by the second day of school and call students by name right away.
4. Stand in your doorway during passing periods to supervise both the hall and your classroom. Do not let students enter or exit through your back door.
5. Provide an opening assignment for students to begin as soon as they enter your classroom.
6. Be sure to enforce all school rules. Failing to do so will make you look weak in the eyes of your students.
7. Always dress in a professional manner. Everything you do makes a statement. If you dress in a casual manner, students might think that you also have a casual attitude about learning. When you dress in a professional manner, you are telling students that you are serious.
8. Be sure to recognize the good work of students. This can be in the form of certificates, positive notes, phone calls to parents, E's in cooperation, or words of praise. Relying only on punishment does not work. You must go out of your way and make it clear to students that you care about them and appreciate their efforts.

Chapter 6

Saturday School

It was 9:15 a.m. on a Saturday. The principal was facing about ninety students in the auditorium. The students had been given Saturday school for breaking school rules.

"Good morning," said the principal. "I am very glad to see you here. Please look up at the front and make eye contact with me."

Once they were all looking at him, the principal began. "First, I want to say that I am very glad to see you here at Saturday school. I am not glad that you got in trouble. But I am glad that you are here today."

The principal walked from side to side in front of the auditorium as he spoke to the students. "My goal is success for each and every one of you," he said. "It is my hope that you will think about some things this morning and figure out some changes that you can make in your life to increase your success."

The principal was doing his best to make eye contact with all of the students. "Your success, more than anything else, will be determined by the decisions you make," he said. "You are the one who controls the decisions you make. That means that you are the one who controls your level of success."

The principal was trying hard to connect with them. "If you can dream it, you can achieve it. That is a reality. And by making good decisions and working hard every day, you can achieve your dreams."

The principal clicked to the second slide of his PowerPoint. "Please look up at the screen," he said. "I will now explain the rules for Saturday school."

* * *

Saturday school is an effective consequence for infractions such as failing to serve detention, habitual tardiness, truancy, and other mid-range infractions.

If it is implemented in a positive manner, it can change an entire school by creating an effective structure that improves student conduct and builds positive attitudes.

The following model for Saturday school focuses on getting students to think about their actions and make positive choices that will improve their success in school. It can handle about one hundred students in an auditorium setting, and it requires three teachers. Students report to Saturday school at 9:00 a.m. and they remain until noon. The morning is divided into three sessions.

During the first session, students check in and go to their assigned seats. They are then told about the rules for Saturday school. Students must treat all others with courtesy, and they are not allowed to talk unless they receive permission.

Students who receive one violation during Saturday school must stay after for five minutes. Students who receive a second violation must stay after for ten minutes. If a student receives three violations, the parent is called and the student is sent home. Saturday school must then be repeated.

After being instructed about the rules of Saturday school, students complete writing assignments in which they are asked to explain the following: (1) Why were you assigned to Saturday school? (2) What will you do to prevent the problem from happening again? (3) What are the benefits of working hard in school? (4) How can you become more successful in school?

During the check-in process, every student is issued a notebook that contains reading materials about making positive choices, taking control of their lives, and thinking about career goals. If students finish their writing assignments early, they are instructed to read in these notebooks. When the first session is over students receive a ten-minute break.

During the second session, students write answers to the following questions aimed at getting them to think about their natural talents and possible career goals: (1) Activities that you enjoy can be a key to your natural talents. What are some activities that you enjoy doing in your spare time? (2) Activities that you can do easily can be a clue to your natural talents. What are some activities that are easy for you? (3) Make a list of the first twenty different jobs that you can think of. Write as quickly as you can. (4) Look at the twenty jobs that you listed. Choose one job that you might enjoy. Why might you enjoy doing that job?

Staff members move about among the students as they are writing to read their assignments and provide encouragement. At the end of this session, one of the staff members gives a motivational speech to the students, which focuses on identifying their natural talents and choosing a career goal that utilizes those talents. When the session is over the students go outside for their second break.

During the third session, students answer the following questions to further develop their goals: (1) It is ten years in the future, and you are working in the career of your dreams. Describe the career of your dreams. (2) If you can dream it, you can achieve it. What can you begin doing now to achieve your dream? (3) You can achieve anything if you are determined, persistent, and courteous. How will those characteristics help you to achieve your dream?

At the conclusion of the third session, students are given an additional pep talk about achieving their dreams. When the session is over, students submit all of their writing assignments. The assignments are then mailed home to their parents.

An effective record-keeping system is needed for all of this to work, and it is very important to have a strong clerical person who is thorough and detail-oriented. This person notifies parents and keeps track of all of the students who are assigned to Saturday school.

Students who fail to report to Saturday school are summoned by a dean to receive a zero-one suspension. In a zero-one suspension, students receive a one-day suspension. However, the suspension is cancelled if the parent comes to school on the following day for a parent conference. This keeps the student in school. It also gets the parent on your side by demonstrating that you are trying to work with the student in a positive way.

Chapter 7

Lunch Supervision

The principal stepped out of his office to the quad. It was 12:40 p.m., and lunch had just begun. It was the second week of October, and the weather was starting to cool off a little bit.

The area behind the outdoor stage looked fine. Students were relaxed and calm. The principal looked toward the north quad, and that was calm too. He quickly stepped into the boys' restroom in the D row. The restroom was also fine.

When the principal looked toward the west quad, there was a problem. About eight Imperials, a Latino gang, were standing near room F-11. This was their normal location. But none of them were smiling, and they looked tense. He then saw three Normandies, an African American gang, walk up to the Imperials. It looked like they were upset about something.

He got on his radio to call for assistance, "503 by room F-11. Two groups. We need a roundup."

Additional supervision staff soon arrived. They escorted the Imperials to room F-11, and the Normandies to room F-12.

* * *

You cannot allow gangs to run your school. This means that you have to be very vigilant and very proactive. You need to know who are gang members. You need to establish close communication with them. You must also establish trust.

If it appears that you are having a gang conflict, the first thing that you must do is isolate both sides and get them into separate rooms. This allows you to identify them and find out what the conflict is about. It also allows you to warn them and inform their parents.

It is very important that you keep a confidential list, with pictures, of suspected gang members. It is important that you develop informants who will give you information about possible gang activity. It is important that you use community gang-prevention agencies to assist you. It is also very important that you work closely with the police department in your community.

Students who become involved with gangs frequently come from dysfunctional families. They do not get the support they need from home, and they frequently use the gang as a substitute for their real family. They want to be successful in life and they want a future. But the older they get, the more at-risk they become. And the more at-risk they become, the more they feel they have nothing to lose.

The gang can become everything to them. And if the gang tells them to fight, they have to fight. If they do not, they will be putting their safety or even their lives at risk. It's a downhill spiral and a tragic mentality of hopelessness.

You must work with gang members in a positive way and do everything you can to help them. This means establishing relationships and really getting to know them. You must also remember that they will fight if their gang tells them to fight.

Chapter 8

A Fight That Was Prevented

It was 3:05 p.m. The dismissal bell had rung. The principal was standing at the front of the school watching the students exit from the main gate. Lunch had been calm, and they were not expecting any problems. It seemed like a nice, calm dismissal.

Five minutes later, the principal noticed two groups exiting the campus. One group was walking behind the other, the students seemed excited, and they were walking faster than usual. Some of the students were talking on their cell phones. The principal had not seen this pattern before, and it appeared suspicious.

The principal got on his radio. "503, main gate. Two groups, about 20 students total, walking west."

As the second group passed him on the sidewalk, the principal started walking behind them. An assistant principal and a campus supervisor joined him. The students walked west across the front of the campus and north up the street. Some of the girls in the groups started taking off their earrings. The adults continued following the students as they walked up the street.

The principal got on his radio again. "This group is still 503, about 20 total. It looks like about four female students getting ready to go 415. They are walking north toward McDonald's."

The assistant principal used his cell phone to call the police. The adults continued following the students.

When the students reached McDonald's, two police cars were already there. The groups broke up and the students walked home. There were no further incidents.

The students had been ready to fight. But the fight had been prevented because of watchful adults who provided strong supervision.

On the following day, key students from both groups were brought into the dean's office. The situation was investigated and the parents were informed. A mediation was also conducted. The conflict was resolved and there was no fighting.

* * *

Students must be closely supervised at all times and in all places. They must be supervised on campus during school, off campus before and after school, and at all school events. Do not take anything for granted when it comes to student safety.

Conflicts between students that are not resolved can quickly escalate. A fight between two individual students on Tuesday can easily become a fight between two groups of students on Wednesday. It goes without saying that students who fight can be seriously injured. And if students decide to bring weapons, somebody can get killed.

What are the important steps for improving supervision? First, look at a map of your campus and the surrounding neighborhood. Meet with police and your security staff to identify trouble areas. Then work together to develop a plan to provide strong supervision. The closer you supervise, including off campus, the safer you will become.

Next, work out a system of radio codes that is easy to understand. Codes such as "415" for a fight and "503" for a near fight are essential. You should also have a code, such as "Code A," if a staff member needs assistance. "Code G" is a good code to use for gang activity.

Make sure that students are carefully supervised during all passing periods. Hall passes, except for discipline referrals or passes to the health office, should be prohibited during the first and last ten minutes of each class period. This is necessary so that you can keep your campus clear and prevent truancy.

It is also important to supervise students very closely during lunch. If you see unusual grouping or sense that students are having a conflict, make a "503" radio call as a signal to round up the students and bring them into a classroom where they can be isolated, identified, and investigated.

Any students who actually fight should be suspended from school for at least one day. During the time of the suspension, each student should write a twenty-page essay describing what happened, apologizing for what happened, and explaining how to resolve any future conflicts in a positive way. The students should also describe their goals in life, the importance of school, and how to be successful in school.

It is not desirable for students to miss school. However, unless you have an in-school suspension program where the students are fully isolated, at-home suspension is needed to help the situation cool off. When the students return from suspension, it is very important that they participate in mediation to ensure that the fighting does not occur again. This is necessary to ensure that the conflict is fully resolved.

Chapter 9

The Problem with Suspensions

A teacher from another school was sitting across from the principal in his office. It was after school. She was interviewing the principal for a class to get her administrative credential.

"So what do you do if a student breaks the rules?" the teacher asked.

"Our main consequence is detention," said the principal. "If a student is tardy at the beginning of the day, he gets one detention. If he is tardy during periods two through six, he gets three detentions. If a student is found out of class without a pass, he gets six detentions."

"How long does each detention last?" the teacher asked.

"Twenty minutes," said the principal. "Students go to our multipurpose room during lunch and write a one-page essay on how to be successful in school."

"What if a student is acting up in class?" the teacher asked.

"The teacher assigns detention for classroom misbehavior," said the principal. "The detention slip gets placed in a special mailbox in the main office, and we enter the detention into a master spreadsheet on Google Docs."

"How do you make sure that students actually serve their detentions?" the teacher asked.

"Through our spreadsheet on Google Docs, we know exactly who owes detention," said the principal. "The spreadsheet can be viewed by the deans, the counselors, and the administrators. If students do not serve detention on their own, we pick them up from their classes before lunch and bring them to the multipurpose room."

"We also increase the length of the writing assignment if students do not serve detention," said the principal. "Instead of a one-page essay on 11-inch paper, students write a two-page essay on 14-inch paper. If the problem persists, we make a special effort to contact the parents."

"How well does it work?" the teacher asked.

"It works better than any other system I know of," said the principal. "It is simple, and the kids know they have to serve detention if it gets assigned to them. Because there is a consistent consequence, students know they must follow the rules."

"How often do you suspend students?" the teacher asked.

"Almost never, unless there is a fight," said the principal. "If there is a fight, we suspend the student for the rest of the current school day and the next school day. We do that to help things cool down."

"What was it like before you went to this system?" the teacher asked.

"It was not good," said the principal. "We used to suspend a lot of kids. I remember one day, when I was a dean about twenty-five years ago, when I suspended fifteen students in one day."

"That's a lot of kids," said the teacher.

"That's how it was back in the old days," said the principal. "And the more we suspended kids, the worse the problems became. We thought we were giving the students a punishment that would make them act better. In reality, we were rewarding them with vacation time if they did wrong. We were also causing them to fall behind academically and give up on themselves even more."

"I can see that," said the teacher.

"We were also sending a very negative message to the parents," said the principal. "We were telling parents that we did not want their kids in school. That is a terrible message to give to parents."

* * *

Suspensions are counterproductive. Instead of making things better, in the long run they make things worse. You should suspend for infractions such as fighting and possession of weapons. You should also call the parents to school and suspend for the rest of the school day if a student is under the influence of a controlled substance. Other than that, you should not suspend.

Keep focusing on what you must do to change a student and create positive attitudes. Do as much as you can to avoid suspensions.

Chapter 10

The First Award of His Entire Life

It was 9:15 a.m. as the principal walked to the library for the monthly awards ceremony. Approximately fifty students had been nominated by their teachers for academic improvement, helping others, and outstanding citizenship.

The principal was carrying a box of medals that had been donated by the school's yearbook vendor. The cost of each medal was $5.00, and the vendor had donated five hundred of them. This would supply the school for one year. Each student would also receive a certificate of recognition detailing the reasons for his or her award.

When the principal got to the library, the students were already waiting for him. The goal was to make the students feel good about their accomplishments and encourage them to continue their efforts.

The ceremony began at 9:30 a.m.

"I am so glad to be here with you this morning," said the principal. "In many cases, your teachers have nominated you because of improvements you have been making. In other cases, you are being recognized for helping others or outstanding citizenship. These qualities are important, because they will bring success to you here at school. They will also bring success to you throughout your entire life."

"Please come forward when I call your name," said the principal.

An individual picture was taken of each student as they received their awards. A group picture, to be posted in the main hallway and placed on the school's website, was also taken.

Students were dismissed to their next classes after the ceremony was concluded. As the principal was walking down the hallway, he overheard one of the recipients talking to his friend.

"I can't believe it," said the student. "This is the first award of my entire life!"

It was a statement of appreciation that the principal would never forget.

* * *

When you provide positive recognition, you are providing a very important element that is essential for improving the way students feel about themselves. Many students do not get enough positive recognition from their parents. These students are thirsty for recognition. When you recognize them for their accomplishments, it can be a life-changing experience for them.

A simple way to provide recognition is to conduct monthly awards ceremonies where teachers nominate students for qualities such as improved academic achievement, outstanding citizenship, and acts of courtesy. These are awards that every student is capable of earning.

When teachers complete their nomination forms, ask them to explain the specific reasons for each award. Then print these reasons on their certificates. If you can combine certificates with medals or simple trophies, the awards can become even more meaningful.

You cannot have too much positive recognition. Everybody needs it. And every student who receives an award can contribute to a ripple effect that has a positive effect on your entire school.

Chapter 11

It Was Almost a Real Emergency

The principal rushed into his office and shut the door. His shirt and pants were muddy. His tie had mud on it. He also had mud in his hair. But at least he hadn't torn anything. He cleaned up in the sink and changed into his spare clothes.

The principal returned to the lunch area as quickly as he could. The students were okay, and it felt like a normal lunch. The chief safety officer came over to the principal's position near the back of the auditorium. They could see most of the lunch area from there.

"Did you see how the fight started?" the officer asked.

"No," said the principal. "By the time I got there, they were already rolling on the ground and pulling each other's hair. I was trying to pull them apart. That's when I fell in the mud." The principal looked around the campus. "Do you know why they were fighting?"

"They bumped into each other as they were going through the gate to the football field," said the officer. "Then they started calling each other names after they got out to the field."

"Was any of the name-calling racial?" the principal asked.

"Yes," said the officer. "They were both doing it."

The principal got on the radio. "This is Z-5. I need everybody on high alert. We are on high alert."

* * *

The fight had started during an earthquake drill. There were several mistakes during the drill that resulted in the fight and caused racial tensions to escalate.

First, some of the gates to the evacuation area had not been opened. This caused a bottleneck at the entrance to the football field. That's where the girls bumped into each other. All of the gates should have been opened immediately after the fire bell started ringing.

Second, the person assigned to the area of the football field where the fight took place had not been there. This contributed to the fight. Supervision assignments should have been reviewed prior to the drill to ensure that all areas were covered.

Third, the emergency drill should not have been scheduled right before lunch. Additional fighting could have occurred very easily during lunch due to the tensions that were caused by the first fight.

When things are safe, it is very easy to get complacent and take that safety for granted. Keep asking yourself what could go wrong and prepare for it. Keep reminding yourself never to take chances with safety or supervision.

Chapter 12

Riot and Recovery

It was the Friday of the third week of February. Lunch had just started. The principal was standing outside near the back corner of the auditorium. From that position, he could see both the quad and the cafeteria lines. The sun was out and it was starting to get warm.

It had been a tough week, with some serious student conflicts.

There had been a gang-related fight on Tuesday evening when a bus carrying students from an occupational training program returned to the school. Approximately thirty students began fighting due to a conflict that had started at the occupational program. The combatants had been gang-related and of different ethnicities. Some of the students had used bats and pipes. One student got his teeth knocked out.

Wednesday had been quiet. There had been no tensions or indications that any additional fighting would occur.

But there had been another serious incident during lunch on Thursday. Fourteen students began fighting behind the cafeteria. The school staff reacted quickly, and all of the participants were apprehended and suspended. Two of them were arrested.

Even though the fighting that week had been gang-related and between students of different ethnicities, the principal believed that the conflict was going to end. There had been no serious gang problems or racial problems previously that year. And all of the students who had fought on Thursday had been suspended. It seemed to the principal that the tensions would be cooled by the following week.

But on Friday, the principal learned that he was wrong.

A Latino student and an African American student began arguing on the quad. The principal intervened to escort the African American student to the office. A safety officer intervened to escort the Latino student to the office.

Then it escalated. A student bystander threw a plastic soda bottle, and suddenly many students were throwing bottles. Numerous fights broke out at the same time. It was a riot.

Everywhere he looked the principal saw fighting. As soon as he would break up one fight, another fight would start. The fighting got worse, and worse, and worse. Students were being attacked solely because of their ethnicity. Nothing the adults could do would stop it.

The students were still fighting when approximately twenty sheriff's deputies arrived. The deputies sent the African American students to the cafeteria and the Latino students to the auditorium. Ten students were arrested. The campus was cleared and the fighting ended.

Period six was cancelled and students were confined to their fifth-period classrooms for the rest of the school day. A controlled dismissal was begun at 2:45 p.m. in which students from four classrooms at a time were escorted to the exit gate. Sheriff's deputies patrolled the streets to keep students moving and prevent them from fighting again.

By 3:45 p.m., the dismissal was completed. The streets were clear, and it was quiet. When the principal returned to his office, he was drained.

Several students received lacerations and bruises. A teacher received a serious injury from being hit in the eye with a plastic soda bottle. It was the principal's worst experience in his twenty-five years as an educator.

* * *

Planning began that weekend to begin the healing process. Supervision procedures were modified to improve security and increase safety. Measures were also taken to improve racial harmony. Tensions gradually eased, and the school returned to normal. The following plans were implemented to improve the climate of the campus:

1. All counselors were assigned to assist with supervision during lunch. Previously, they had been allowed to remain in their offices.
2. The district provided additional funding to pay for teachers to provide lunch supervision.
3. Two staff members carrying video cameras were assigned to provide supervision during lunch. They were instructed to film any conflicts or fighting that took place. The cameras provided a strong deterrent.
4. Two large rooms near the central part of the lunch area were identified as places where students could be isolated if tensions began to develop. Students who were brought to these rooms would remain for the remainder of lunch. They would be identified, and ID photos would be taken

if necessary. These students would also be searched for possible gang identification.
5. All sales of drinks from plastic bottles were suspended.
6. Stronger supervision was provided each evening at 7:00 p.m. when the bus from the regional occupation center returned to school.
7. Lunch was shortened from thirty-five minutes to thirty minutes. This provided less idle time for students.
8. Special meetings were conducted for parents and teachers to discuss the situation and announce the plans for increased security.
9. Campus lockdown plans were modified to include procedures that took into account a double-lunch bell schedule. The previous lockdown plan had been based on a single-lunch bell schedule.
10. A grab-and-go plan was implemented for any future disturbances. If fighting broke out, members of the security staff would grab a fighter, bring the fighter to the isolation room, and secure him there before going to apprehend any other fighters.
11. A stronger effort was made through rewards and incentives to improve the network of student informants. This provided much better information for preventing future problems.
12. Campus publicity was increased for the peer mediation program. Posters were placed throughout the campus to publicize the program.
13. A student club was created that focused on improving racial harmony. This was sponsored by some very dedicated teachers who were outstanding role models.
14. An assembly for Black History Month was held during the following week. It was organized by two outstanding teachers, one Latino and one African American. The assembly focused on racial harmony and respect for others. The teachers who organized the assembly modeled unity, and the students reacted very positively.

It was a terrible riot that did a great deal of damage. Luckily, the school was able to recover. The lesson from this is that you must never underestimate the seriousness of gang activity or racial tensions. Keep your finger on the pulse of your campus. Keep asking yourself how to get better. And do not take safety for granted.

Chapter 13

Section Review

Effective discipline is the foundation of a school. If you have strong discipline, you can move forward with the elements necessary for every student to learn at high levels. If you do not have strong discipline, the learning will suffer.

High standards of behavior are needed for high standards of learning. The following elements will bring about effective, school-wide discipline:

1. Provide a simple set of school rules that everybody can remember.
2. Provide meaningful and fair consequences that are enforced with one hundred percent consistency by all staff members.
3. Work with counselors, deans, and administrators to ensure they have strong skills for working with parents and students.
4. Provide positive recognition for students who are doing a good job.
5. Supervise carefully and plan ahead for emergencies.

Implementation of these elements allows you to create a positive and supportive school culture where teachers can focus on teaching and students can focus on learning. This creates a foundation that makes it possible for every student to learn at high levels.

CLASSROOM INSTRUCTION

Chapter 14

The Learning in Classrooms

The principal could not hear anything as he unlocked the door. When he went inside, he saw that all of the students had their textbooks open and were doing assignments. It was a U.S. history class. The learning standard was posted on the board, and there were meaningful subject-matter displays on the walls. The room was neat and orderly.

The principal's first reaction was positive, because the engagement level seemed high. But as he walked around the room he saw that students were answering questions at the back of the chapter by copying sentences from the chapter. The reading was about the period leading up to the Civil War. The principal bent down and asked a female student to explain what the assignment was about. She said that she did not know.

The principal's next classroom was English 9. It was noisy as he unlocked the door, and he expected to see problems. But when he walked inside, he saw that students were learning at high levels. The students had all written essays, and they were sitting in pairs reading them aloud to each other.

The principal sat down with one of the pairs and listened to them as they read their essays. They had written reactions to a short story they had read, and they were excited.

The teacher raised his hand, and the room became quiet. "This is step two," he said. "When I give the word you will trade papers with the person sitting in the row next to you. Mark a straight line under the areas that are written clearly. Mark a curvy line under areas that are hard to understand or that might have grammar mistakes."

The teacher began to check for understanding by calling on randomly selected students and providing ten seconds of wait time after each question.

"With whom will you trade your paper?" the teacher asked. Ten seconds passed. "Joseph?"

"The person sitting next to me," said Joseph. "That will be Bobby."
"What kind of a line will you place under sections that are written clearly?" the teacher asked. Ten seconds passed. "Maria?"
"A straight line," said Maria.
"What kind of a line will you place under sections that need clarification?" the teacher asked. Ten seconds passed. "Sonia?"
"A curvy line," said Sonia.
"There will be no talking until I give the word," said the teacher. "I want full concentration. Ready, go."
The students traded papers silently and began working.

* * *

Instructional leadership means keeping yourself focused on classrooms and instruction. How do you do that? First, you have to schedule your time to make sure that you and your administrators get into classrooms to observe for at least one hour every day. You must also spend the time that is necessary to meet with teachers and provide feedback.

In the first classroom, there were serious problems. The room looked good and the students were cooperative and quiet. But they were doing mindless busywork. The next job with such a classroom is to visit again during another class period. After that, if there is still a problem, you should place a note in the teacher's mailbox asking the teacher to meet with you in your office on the following day.

The reason for visiting again is to give yourself a clearer picture so that you don't jump to conclusions about what is happening in the classroom. The reason for meeting with the teacher in your office is to provide a setting that is private and respectful of the teacher. The reason for meeting on the following day is to give yourself time to collect your thoughts so that you do not say something that will make the situation worse.

The second classroom had numerous examples of excellent instruction. The lesson was well planned and standards based. Thinking skills were being addressed at high levels. The teacher ensured full participation by having students read each other's papers. The teacher also checked for understanding by calling on students who were randomly selected.

You should meet with this teacher on the following day to provide positive feedback. Make sure that you tell this teacher that he or she is doing an excellent job. You should also encourage the teacher to make his or her classroom available for visits by other teachers.

All of this takes a great deal of time, and it's a slow process. But most improvements take place through a series of small steps. It's a growing process that you must engage in every day. Teachers feel supported when you visit classrooms. You also demonstrate to students that learning is your top priority.

If you and your administrators are observing instruction and meeting with teachers every day, you will see significant improvements in student achievement. Every time you visit classrooms and meet with teachers, you are helping to improve the learning at your school.

Chapter 15

The Reason It Worked

The bell rang and the students were all in class. The principal walked down the length of the first floor and everything was quiet. He opened the door to room 103 and went inside. It was the first time he had visited that room during sustained silent reading.

Everybody was reading, including the teacher. The room was totally silent. The students were all fully engaged. The principal sat down in the back and opened his book. There was full concentration on reading by everybody in the classroom.

Twenty minutes later, the bell rang. The teacher stood up from her desk. "Jose, what did you read?"

"It's a story that takes place right after World War II," said Jose. "The main character is a guy named Richard. He was a soldier in the army. When he comes back home, he can't adjust to normal life. He keeps having flashbacks of a battle where his best friend was killed right in front of him. His hands are always shaking and he loses his temper all the time."

The teacher spoke again. "Beth, what did you read?"

"It's about this girl in the eighth grade and everything that she goes through," said Beth. "Her family is all messed up. Her mom is trying to keep the family together. But her older brother is in jail for stealing a car. The part that I read talked about how the mom might lose her job because the store where she works might go out of business."

The teacher got up from her desk and went to the overhead projector. "Good job. Please open page 82."

When the principal left the classroom, he felt so good inside. All of the students had been highly engaged in their books. The teacher had been reading her book. And when the teacher randomly called on the students to explain what they had read, their answers indicated that their comprehension levels were high and they were interested in what they were reading.

* * *

You must always remember that it is people who solve problems, not programs. You must also remember that the best way to solve a problem is to address it directly.

A sustained silent reading program, if it is done properly with thorough and collaborative planning, is an effective way to directly improve reading skills. It increases student engagement with reading. This, in turn, improves fluency and comprehension. But you will not accomplish anything if it is not implemented properly.

The first step is to check the research. You should never ask teachers to do anything unless it is research-based. And be sure to look for empirical research. There is a lack of empirical research on the effectiveness of sustained silent reading. However, there is extensive empirical research on the relationship between academic engagement time and learning. If students are genuinely engaged in reading, their reading skills will improve.

The next step is to thoroughly involve teachers in the planning. This takes advantage of their expertise so that the program works effectively. You should meet with an initial planning group, such as department chairs, to create a basic plan. This will probably take two or three meetings.

Next, you should present the plan developed by this planning group to all teachers. A good way to do this is to have conference-period faculty meetings so that teachers are able to discuss the plan and ask questions.

You should present the plan to students so you can get their ideas. An effective way of doing this is to meet with a focus group of ten or fifteen randomly selected students, as well as representatives from your student council. You should also present the plan for discussion during parent meetings.

After the plan has been revised based upon the input of teachers, students, and parents, you should discuss it once more with your initial planning group. You should then schedule a kick-off date and publicize the plan through posters, public address announcements, and written notices.

Once the program begins, it is very important that you follow up every day to ensure that it is being implemented fully. For example, with sustained silent reading you should briefly look into three or four classrooms at the beginning of each reading period to check for implementation.

Next, you should stay in one of the classrooms to read along with the students. This demonstrates your support for the program and provides a way for you to be a positive role model. It also gives you an opportunity at the end of each reading period to give students a pep talk about the value of reading.

If the teacher is having trouble implementing the program, you should meet with the teacher and provide assistance as soon as possible.

Why does a program such as sustained silent reading really work? It is not about the program. It is about the people and their belief in the program. It works because teachers, students, and parents were involved in planning the solution. It works because of the dedication and skill of teachers. It works because of a committed principal who goes into classrooms to make sure it is implemented properly.

Chapter 16

A Sustained Process

It was the third week of November. The bell to begin sustained silent reading had rung ten minutes earlier. The principal was on the west side of the campus, getting ready to observe in his third classroom. The first two classrooms had been great, and the principal felt very encouraged.

Unfortunately, it didn't last. As the principal stood outside the door of the third classroom, he heard excessive talking. He turned his key and entered through the back door. This would be his first observation of that teacher.

About a third of the students were socializing, and they were very loud. Approximately ten students were texting or listening to their iPods. Three students were doing homework. Only five students were engaged in sustained silent reading.

The teacher was sitting at the front of the classroom, looking at his computer. He did not look up or seem to notice when the principal entered the classroom.

When the principal reached the front of the classroom, he noticed that the teacher was reading Sports Illustrated on his computer. The principal moved to the rear of the classroom and sat down at an empty desk to complete the notes for a classroom observation report.

The principal met with the teacher on the following day. He opened the meeting by giving the teacher a copy of the observation report.

"When I entered your classroom yesterday, I observed that five of the students were engaged in sustained silent reading," said the principal. "Sixteen students appeared to socializing, three of students were doing homework, and ten students were listening to music or texting. The noise level from the students who were talking was pretty high."

"I knew there was some talking," said the teacher. "But I didn't think it was that bad. I allow the students to work on their homework, because that is a form of reading."

"When I first came into your classroom, you did not seem to be aware that I had entered," said the principal. "When I looked at your computer screen, I saw that you were reading Sports Illustrated."

"It surprised me when I saw you next to my desk, because I had not heard the door open," said the teacher. "The reason why I was reading Sports Illustrated is because I was reading along with the students for sustained silent reading. I did not think it would be a problem."

"Have you met the new assistant principal?" the principal asked. "I think you would enjoy working with her."

"She seems very nice," said the teacher. "But I have not spoken with her individually."

"I will ask her to come and see you," said the principal. "Please remember that during sustained silent reading, every student must be reading a book of his or her choice. In addition, as a role model, it is very important that you are also reading a book. Every student must be reading for the entire twenty minutes."

"I understand," said the teacher.

* * *

This was an experienced teacher, possibly near retirement, who should have been implementing sustained silent reading. Instead, he was letting the students have free time. Why was this happening?

The principal found out that the teacher had a history of assigning extensive written work instead of providing activities that involved discussion or direct instruction. The assignments usually given by the teacher lacked rigor and did little to develop thinking skills. In addition, the teacher gave most of his students an A or a B. There was a serious lack of rigor. And it had been happening for a long time.

It seemed possible to the principal that the teacher might also have a hearing problem. This was based upon the teacher's lack of awareness that the students in the class were talking loud. It might also explain the lack of discussion activities.

Finally, the principal wondered if the teacher was just going through the motions, waiting for retirement.

What are the next steps?

It is important to discuss the situation with your supervisor. Maybe a staff member from your district office is available to work closely with the teacher. If not, you need to identify a person from your school to provide assistance.

After a second observation, if you still think there might be a hearing problem, you need to meet with the teacher and have a discussion about getting his hearing tested.

It is also necessary to observe the teacher frequently. This means classroom observations at least once a month, with individual meetings that include written feedback.

This is a sustained process, not a quick fix. It needs to happen in a positive manner, so that the teacher knows you are genuinely trying to help him. In addition, be sure you are communicating frequently with your supervisor about the teacher.

Hopefully, the teacher will improve. In reality, however, he might not. If improvement is not noted after numerous observations and feedback, the principal needs to consider giving a below-standard evaluation.

Chapter 17

He Had Firmly Believed

It was his second year as a principal, and he was so disappointed. The faculty had just voted down block scheduling for the second time. When the teachers had voted on block scheduling the previous year, the vote had been close. But the results of the second vote were clearly against block scheduling.

The school would now be staying with a standard six-period school day. The principal had firmly believed that block scheduling would significantly improve student achievement. The vote was a tremendous setback to him.

* * *

It was his eighth year as a principal. He had just been assigned to a new school, and it was the third Friday of September. The dismissal bell had rung. The administrators, deans, and counselors were supervising in front of the campus. It had been a block-scheduling day, with 120-minute class periods.

An assistant principal walked over and stood next to the principal. "Are you okay?" the assistant principal asked. "You look like you had a bad day."

"I went into ten classrooms today," said the principal. "Two of them were excellent. The teachers were working hard and the students were learning at high levels. But in eight of the classrooms, the teachers were showing entertainment videos. There was no learning going on."

The principal looked down the street to check for problems. "Eight classrooms!" he said. "I saw everything from 'It's a Wonderful Life,' to 'Lethal Weapon.' I also saw a movie in Spanish with a car chase and a gun battle. It was so disappointing."

The principal paused and looked down the street again. "When I got here I was so excited about the block scheduling you already had here," he said. "I thought that longer class periods were the answer for bringing about better teaching. But that is not the case. I learned a lot today."

* * *

It is so important that we improve our schools. And when a new program looks promising, many people get excited and embrace the program. They believe that the program is the solution that will help every student learn better.

But it is not about programs. It is about the people who use the programs. It is about skilled and dedicated teachers who are working with students and striving to help them learn better through good, solid, effective teaching.

You can take the greatest program in the world, and an unskilled teacher can ruin it in about fifteen minutes. But you can take the worst program in the world, and a skilled teacher who cares can make it work under the most difficult circumstances.

You will never find the answers to improving student achievement by simply chasing after new programs. But you will find the answers by observing in classrooms, identifying the real problems, understanding the research, and working with your staff.

It is people who solve problems, not programs.

You need clear standards to guide teachers so they know what to teach. You need ways to measure the learning that is taking place. You also need time during work hours for teachers to meet together, look at the research, share ideas, and learn from each other.

New programs are tempting. But they are not necessarily the answer.

You need the strength, the courage, and the wisdom to observe in classrooms, work with teachers, and focus on solutions that are research based. You will not improve learning by simply implementing new programs.

Chapter 18

You Have to Go Out and Look for Problems

The principal opened the door at the back of the classroom and went inside. It was a ninth-grade English class with an enrollment of about twenty students. He had expected to see a successful lesson. But that is not what he saw.

Most of the students were socializing. Some of them were walking around the classroom and talking. Some were sitting at their desks and talking. Some were texting on their cell phones. A few had their heads down, as if they were sleeping.

The teacher was sitting at her desk at the front of the classroom. When she asked the students to be quiet, they ignored her. When she asked them to do the assignment written on the whiteboard, they ignored her. She made no effort to correct their behavior. The socializing and the noise continued.

The principal sat down at a desk at the rear of the classroom and continued looking around. The room was filthy. He saw textbooks, empty bags of chips, and plastic soda bottles thrown on the floor. The desktop where he sat was covered with gang graffiti and drawings of sex acts. He saw additional gang graffiti marked on the bulletin boards. He saw gang graffiti written on the walls.

He had not expected to see this. Whenever he had seen the teacher on the campus or in the office, she had seemed happy. She had not been known for sending students out of her classroom with discipline referrals. She had never complained. From the few times the principal had spoken with her, he knew that she was a person who really cared about kids.

When the principal met with her after the visit, she told him that she had been afraid to ask for help because she was a second-year teacher and she thought it would jeopardize her job.

The principal assigned an instructional coach to work with the teacher and provide intensive support. Sadly, however, the teacher did not improve.

The principal did not request a renewal of her contract for the following school year.

* * *

You will not improve your school by assuming that things are going well or waiting for people to ask for help. You have to go out and look for problems.

Your top priority must be classroom instruction, and you should be in classrooms constantly. Don't fall into a pattern where you are only visiting classrooms at certain times of the day. And keep a list to make sure you are getting into all of the classrooms.

You must also be thinking about everything else at your school that could go wrong. You must go into restrooms to make sure they are clean. You must inspect your athletics facilities and make sure that your coaches have first-aid kits. You must supervise your campus carefully and know your trouble spots. You must check financial procedures and monitor your budgets.

People are not always going to ask for help if they are having difficulties. You have to aggressively go out and look for problems. Every problem that you solve will make your school better. The quicker you discover a problem, the quicker you can fix it.

Chapter 19

The Best Way to Spend Your Time

It was 4:00 p.m. on Monday when the principal received the telephone call. It was the district office. A parent had complained that her son had not gotten a textbook in his English class. The teacher had been directed verbally during the previous week to issue all textbooks.

* * *

It was 11:00 a.m. on Tuesday when the principal received the telephone call. It was a parent. Somebody had broken into her son's physical education locker and stolen $80 that he had brought to buy his yearbook. The theft had happened during the student's physical education class. The locker room should have been secured. It was the fifth complaint in a month about a theft from the boys' locker room.

* * *

It was 9:30 a.m. on Wednesday when the principal received the radio call. Somebody had lit off a firework inside a classroom. When the principal got to the classroom, the teacher said that he had not seen who had lit it. There had been problems in that room all year.

* * *

It was 4:30 p.m. on Thursday when the principal received the telephone call. It was another parent. She complained that a teacher had called her daughter "stupid." The daughter had come home crying. This was the second complaint that the principal had received about the teacher. The teacher had already been written up once.

* * *

Most of the problems at your school are not going to happen in your office. They are going to happen on your campus and in classrooms. The more you are out on your campus and in classrooms, the more you are being preventive. The more you are in your office, the more you are being reactive.

By getting out on your campus and visiting classrooms, you are accomplishing three things. First, you are finding out what is really happening. This makes it possible for you to identify problems quicker and take action when problems are still small. It also helps you to make better decisions.

Next, you are providing encouragement to those who are doing a good job. Teaching is a lonely profession, and by going into classrooms, you are showing teachers that you care about their teaching. It also shows students that you care about their learning.

Finally, you are keeping people on their toes. Almost all of your visits to classrooms should be unannounced. That way you know that what you are seeing is real. It also demonstrates to teachers that you have high expectations.

The more reactive you are—staying in your office and taking on problems only when they reach your desk—the more problems you will have. The more proactive you are by going out on your campus and visiting classrooms, the more problems you will prevent.

Chapter 20

It Was His First Day

It was mid-October. The principal and the new teacher were sitting in the principal's office. The enrollment had gone up, and they were adding another English teacher. The principal had written out an orientation schedule for the new teacher on the previous afternoon.

"This is your schedule for the next two days," said the principal. "I want you to observe a variety of good teachers so you can see a variety of successful teaching strategies."

"This is a lot of visits," said the teacher.

"By going into these classrooms, you will get a good feel for the school," said the principal. "You will also get to know some of our strongest teachers. And they will become your support system."

"Great!"

The principal came to the teacher's side of the desk so he could explain the materials better. "This is a copy of our school map," said the principal. "It also has our bell schedule. During lunch, our faculty cafeteria is here."

The principal turned to the next page of the teacher's schedule. "You will be visiting classrooms for the entire day today," said the principal. "I want you to see a variety of instructional strategies. Two of the teachers are in the English Department. You will also be visiting teachers in math, chemistry, and history."

"Tomorrow you will observe the chairperson of the English Department," said the principal. You will also see another math teacher, and an art teacher. You will see some excellent instruction in their classrooms."

"Is there anything else?" the teacher asked.

"During period four today, I have scheduled you to return to this office so I can spend some time with you on classroom discipline," said the principal. "The purpose of this is to help you to get off to the best start possible."

"I really appreciate your help," said the teacher.

"It is also very important that you eat lunch every day in the faculty cafeteria," said the principal. "Some of the teachers in there will say negative things. But you can learn from all of them. And you will need them around you as a support system."

"Anything else?" the teacher asked.

"We interviewed a lot of teacher candidates before selecting you," said the principal. "We all felt that you were the best. I feel that you have the potential to be a great teacher. That's why you were chosen."

* * *

Don't ever forget how hard it is to be a new teacher. Do everything you can to support them. And do everything you can to help them get a good start.

If you invest properly in your teachers, you will get good results. If you fail to support them, you will get terrible results. And you will hurt the students.

Chapter 21

An Opinion Is Not Research

It was his fourth year as a principal. He was sitting near the front at a conference for educators from throughout the state. The keynote speaker was talking about an exciting new program he had developed to improve learning. The program sounded great. He was a very good salesman.

The principal knew that the speaker was sincere and wanted the best for every student. But the principal also knew the research.

The opinion of the speaker was that the new program would improve learning. He believed in the program with all his heart. And he cited anecdotal evidence and the opinions of others as support.

But there was no valid or reliable research to support him. The speaker was giving his opinion. But his opinion was not supported by research.

* * *

Opinion-based programs to improve student achievement often sound good. But they are frequently off target. These programs distract teachers from focusing on research-based strategies that really do improve learning.

Instead of concentrating on strategies to improve student achievement that are validated by research, teachers waste instructional time by focusing on programs that sound good but have questionable value.

Teachers need to use instructional strategies that are supported by valid, reliable research. They need learning standards to guide them in what they are required to teach. They need orderly school environments so that they can fully engage students in learning. During teaching, they need to check for understanding in ways that give them accurate feedback and help to engage all students. They also need time to meet with their colleagues, examine research, and share instructional techniques.

Working with teachers and keeping them focused on research-based strategies takes patience. At first, the improvements in learning may not be apparent. But over time, the improvements will become very evident. Learning will improve because teachers will be focusing their efforts on strategies that really do improve student achievement, not theories that are unproven.

When somebody tells you about a new program that improves student achievement, ask to see the research. You will not have success by asking teachers to focus their efforts on strategies that are opinion-based. You will have success by asking teachers to focus on strategies that are research based.

Chapter 22

Your Presence in Classrooms

It was about 6:00 p.m. on a day in April. The principal walked up the steps to the faculty cafeteria. About 20 parents were present for a PTA meeting. It was the principal's first year at the school, and a lot of improvements were still needed. After the call to order and the reading of the minutes, the principal stood up and went to the front to give an update.

"We are making final preparations to get ready for testing," said the principal. "Last year during testing, students were assigned to classrooms alphabetically, based upon their last names. This caused problems, because in many cases the teachers did not know the students." The principal paused briefly to look around the room and make eye contact. "This year, students will remain with their first-period teachers for the testing," he said. "This will provide a better setting for them to be successful, because the teachers will know them."

A parent raised her hand. "What are you seeing in the classrooms?" she asked. "Last year the principal never left his office."

"I am getting into classrooms every day," said the principal. "I am seeing high standards of student conduct. I am also seeing quality instruction. I get a positive feeling when I walk around the campus. Students seem relaxed and happy."

Another parent raised her hand. "My daughter said that you came into her English class yesterday," she said. "The students were noisy, but when you came into the room they got quiet. My daughter said that you gave them a pep talk and said you believed in them. Two weeks ago, she said you were in her social studies class. So I know what you are saying is true."

* * *

If you cannot do anything else, make sure that you get into classrooms. It is a powerful way to provide leadership. The benefits are almost immeasurable.

First, getting into classrooms helps you to find out what is happening instructionally. This gives you a true picture of the teaching that students are experiencing every day. Your observations will help you to determine the improvements that are most needed.

Next, teachers feel supported when you get into their classrooms. It shows that you care about their efforts. And they will respect your feedback.

Students notice when you get into classrooms. It shows that you care about them, and that you care about learning. Actions speak louder than words. Every time you get into a classroom, you are making a powerful statement that learning is your top priority.

Parents also find out when you get into classrooms. Your presence in classrooms shows that you care about the students, that you know what is going on, and that you are trying to make improvements. This increases their confidence in you as a leader.

Chapter 23

Will It Help Students Learn Better?

It was 11:00 a.m. When the principal got back to his office, he had several phone messages. He had a stack of conference attendance forms that he had to sign, as well as several requisitions. He also had a memo from the district office stating that an attendance report was due.

He left the office and went down the hall to visit classrooms. He would complete the paperwork and phone calls after school.

* * *

You will not achieve success as a principal by staying in your office, talking on the phone, and doing paperwork. You will achieve success by being out on your campus, visiting classrooms, and working with teachers.

Every time you discipline yourself to focus on issues that will help students learn better, you are going in the right direction and spending your time wisely. Every time you let yourself get bogged down in tasks that will have little effect on learning, you are wasting resources and holding your school back from getting better.

Chapter 24

The Power of a Positive Learning Environment

It was 10:00 a.m. The principal was talking to a group of about fifty alumni in the auditorium. He had just finished taking them on a tour of the campus. Most of the alumni had graduated in the 1940s, the 1950s, or the 1960s. The school looked great, and the principal was proud of what they had seen.

"We are working very hard to improve student achievement," said the principal. "I am proud of the improvements we have made, and I am proud of our students. We are better this year than we were last year."

"My goal is for us to have constant improvement," said the principal. "I want us to keep getting better every day, every week, and every year. Are there any questions that I can answer?"

A gentleman sitting near the middle of the audience raised his hand. "Do you really think that all kids can learn?"

The principal felt absolutely crushed. How could anybody ask such a question?

* * *

Students respond to their environment. If you put them in a positive learning environment with skilled teachers who believe in them and have the necessary resources, they will succeed. If you put students in a negative learning environment with unskilled teachers, poor resources, and poor leadership, they will fail.

If you believe that you will succeed, you will succeed. If you believe that you will fail, you will fail.

In many cases, students experience learning difficulties and get negative attitudes about themselves because of problems that started when they were very young. When things go wrong and students have trouble in school, they often come to believe that they are not smart. That's why believing in students and building positive attitudes is so important.

All students can achieve at high levels if they are placed in a positive learning environment with skilled adults who believe in them.

Chapter 25

The Common Core State Standards

It was late April. The district meeting had ended. The principal was walking out to his car in the parking lot. It was a warm afternoon, about eighty degrees.

An administrator from the school district began walking next to the principal. The principal and the administrator had known each other for a long time. "So what do you think about the Common Core State Standards?" asked the administrator.

"I am excited," said the principal. "They are going to help our kids learn at much higher levels and truly get prepared for college."

"Aren't you worried about how to implement them?" asked the administrator.

"I don't think it will be as difficult as people think," said the principal. "For each subject area, I think we need to put the standards into a concise format that fits on two sheets of paper. After that, we need to provide staff development on the standards. Then we ask teachers to post the standards in their classrooms and align their teaching to them."

"Have you seen the new standards?" asked the administrator. "Do you know how long and complicated they are? They are very different from the standards we have now."

"That's why we need to get them into a concise format," said the principal. "We need to put the standards into a format that teachers, students, and parents can all understand."

"What did you think about that sample test they gave us in math?" asked the administrator.

"That's another great way to communicate the standards," said the principal. "Teachers are smart. If you show them the test, they will figure out how to teach to the test. The new standards are going to help teachers address thinking skills at a much higher level."

"How long do you think it will take to make the change, to get the standards fully implemented?" asked the administrator.

"I think it will take about ten years," said the principal. *"We just need to get organized, go step by step, and be patient. This is a massive change that will take time. Our society needs thinkers who know how to find information and understand it, think creatively, and solve problems. This is the right change, and I am excited."*

* * *

The Common Core State Standards are the standards we need to help all students learn at the highest levels. Our students need to become thinkers. First, they need the ability to find information and fully understand it. Next, they need the ability to think creatively and use the information to solve problems.

An important key to implementing the standards is to put them into a concise format. If you try to implement the Common Core Standards by giving teachers numerous articles and books to read, there will be a great deal of confusion. Teachers will become frustrated, and the process will become bogged down.

But if you clearly organize what you want the teachers to teach, put the standards into a concise format, and show teachers what students will be tested on, you will eventually reach a high level of implementation. Step by step, you will achieve success.

The following materials provide examples of how the Common Core State Standards for a high school can be formatted in a concise way that is easier for teachers to use. The standards cover the core subjects of English language arts, mathematics, science, and social studies. Standards for the arts, health, physical education, and world languages are also included. Each set of standards fits on two pages.

COMMON CORE STATE STANDARDS: ENGLISH LANGUAGE ARTS

Key Reading Standards

1. Cite evidence to support analysis of what the text says explicitly and what it infers.
2. Determine two or more central ideas and analyze their development. Provide an objective summary of the text.
3. Analyze a complex set of ideas or sequence of events. Explain how specific individuals, ideas, or events interact and develop.

4. Determine the meanings of words and phrases as they are used in the text, including figurative, connotative, and technical meanings.
5. Analyze and evaluate the effectiveness of the structure an author uses, including whether the structure makes points clear, convincing, and engaging.
6. Determine an author's point of view or purpose. Analyze how style and content contribute to the power, persuasiveness, and beauty of text.
7. Integrate and evaluate multiple sources of information to address a question or solve a problem.
8. Delineate and evaluate the reasoning of seminal U.S. texts, including the application of constitutional principles and the use of legal reasoning.
9. Analyze seminal U.S. documents of historical and literary significance for their themes, purposes, and rhetorical features.
10. Read and comprehend fiction and nonfiction independently and proficiently.

Key Writing Standards

1. Write arguments to support claims using valid reasoning and relevant evidence. Develop arguments precisely, fairly, and clearly. Establish and maintain a formal style and objective tone. Provide a concluding statement that supports the argument presented.
2. Write informative text to examine and convey complex ideas. Develop topics thoroughly. Use precise language with appropriate and varied transitions and syntax. Provide a concluding statement.
3. Write narratives to describe events using effective technique, well-chosen details, and well-structured event sequences. Use precise words and phrases to convey a vivid picture of events.
4. Produce clear and coherent writing in which the development, organization, and style are appropriate to the task, purpose, and audience.
5. Develop and strengthen writing as needed by planning, revising, editing, rewriting, or trying a new approach, focusing on what is most significant for a specific purpose or audience.
6. Use technology, including the Internet, to produce, publish, and update individual and shared writing products.
7. Conduct short as well as sustained research projects to answer questions or solve problems.
8. Gather relevant information from multiple print and digital sources. Assess the strengths and limitations of various sources.
9. Draw evidence from literary and informational texts to support analysis, reflection, and research.

10. Write routinely over extended and shorter time frames for a range of tasks, purposes, and audiences.

Key Speaking and Listening Standards

1. Initiate and participate effectively in collaborative discussions with diverse partners. Build on the ideas of others and express ideas clearly and persuasively.
2. Integrate multiple sources of information in diverse formats to make informed decisions and solve problems.
3. Evaluate a speaker's point of view, reasoning, and use of evidence.
4. Present information, findings, and supporting evidence to convey perspectives and logical arguments. Use appropriate eye contact, adequate volume, and clear pronunciation.
5. Make strategic use of digital media in presentations to enhance understanding and findings.
6. Adapt speech to a variety of contexts and tasks, demonstrating a command of formal English.

Key Language Standards

1. Demonstrate command of standard English grammar and usage when writing and speaking.
2. Demonstrate command of standard English capitalization, punctuation, and spelling.
3. Apply knowledge of language to understand how it functions in different contexts.
4. Determine and clarify the meanings of unknown or multiple-meaning words and phrases.
5. Demonstrate the understanding of figurative language, word relationships, and nuances in word meanings.
6. Acquire and use words and phrases sufficient for reading, writing, and speaking at the college- and career-readiness level.

COMMON CORE STATE STANDARDS: MATHEMATICS

Standards for Mathematical Practice

1. Make sense of problems and persevere in solving them.
2. Reason abstractly and quantitatively.
3. Construct viable arguments and critique the reasoning of others.

4. Model with mathematics.
5. Use appropriate tools strategically.
6. Attend to precision.
7. Look for and make use of structure.
8. Look for and express regularity in repeated reasoning.

Number and Quantity

1. The Real Number System: Extend the properties of exponents to rational exponents. Use properties of rational and irrational numbers.
2. Quantities: Reason quantitatively and use units to solve problems.
3. The Complex Number System: Perform arithmetic operations with complex numbers. Represent complex numbers and their operations on the complex plane. Use complex numbers in polynomial identities and equations.
4. Vector and Matrix Quantities: Represent and model with vector quantities. Perform operations on vectors. Perform operations on matrices and use matrices in applications.

Algebra

1. Seeing Structure in Expressions: Interpret the structure of expressions. Write expressions in equivalent forms to solve problems.
2. Arithmetic and Polynomials and Rational Expressions: Perform arithmetic operations on polynomials. Understand the relationship between zeroes and factors of polynomials. Use polynomial identities to solve problems. Rewrite rational expressions.
3. Creating Equations: Create equations that describe numbers or relationships.
4. Reasoning with Equations and Inequalities: Understand solving equations as a process of reasoning and explain the reasoning. Solve equations and inequalities in one variable. Solve systems of equations. Represent and solve equations and inequalities graphically.

Functions

1. Interpreting Functions: Understand the concept of a function and use function notation. Interpret functions that arise in applications in terms of the context. Analyze functions using different representations.
2. Building Functions: Build a function that models a relationship between two quantities. Build new functions from existing functions.

3. Linear, Quadratic, and Exponential Models: Construct and compare linear, quadratic, and exponential models and solve problems. Interpret expressions for functions in terms of the situation they model.
4. Trigonometric Functions: Extend the domain of trigonometric functions using the unit circle. Model periodic phenomena with trigonometric functions. Prove and apply trigonometric identities.

Geometry

1. Congruence: Experiment with transformations in the plane. Understand congruence in terms of rigid motions. Prove geometric theorems. Make geometric constructions.
2. Similarity, Right Triangles, and Trigonometry: Understand similarity in terms of similarity transformations. Prove theorems involving similarity. Define trigonometric ratios and solve problems involving right triangles. Apply trigonometry to general triangles.
3. Circles: Understand and apply theorems about circles. Find arc lengths and areas of sectors of circles.
4. Expressing Geometric Properties with Equations: Translate between the geometric description and the equation for a conic section. Use coordinates to prove simple geometric theorems algebraically.
5. Geometric Measurement and Dimension: Explain volume formulas and use them to solve problems. Visualize relationships between two-dimensional and three-dimensional objects.
6. Modeling with Geometry: Apply geometric concepts in modeling situations.

Statistics and Probability

1. Interpreting Categorical and Quantitative Data: Summarize, represent, and interpret data on a single count or measurement variable. Summarize, represent, and interpret data on two categorical and quantitative variables. Interpret linear models.
2. Making Inferences and Justifying Conclusions: Understand and evaluate random processes underlying statistical experiments. Make inferences and justify conclusions from sample surveys, experiments, and observational studies.
3. Conditional Probability and the Rules of Probability: Understand independence and conditional probability and use them to interpret data. Use the rules of probability to compute probabilities of compound events in a uniform probability model.

4. Using Probability to Make Decisions: Calculate expected values and use them to solve problems. Use probability to evaluate outcomes of decisions.

COMMON CORE STATE STANDARDS: SCIENCE

Key Reading Standards

1. Cite specific textual evidence to support the analysis of science texts, attending to important distinctions made by the author.
2. Determine the central ideas or conclusions of a text. Summarize complex concepts, processes, or information by paraphrasing in simpler but still accurate terms.
3. Follow complex, multistep procedures when carrying out experiments, taking measurements, or performing technical tasks. Analyze results based upon explanations in the text.
4. Determine the meanings of symbols, key terms, and other domain-specific words and phrases as they are used in scientific contexts.
5. Analyze how a text structures information or ideas into categories or hierarchies, thereby demonstrating understanding of the information or ideas.
6. Analyze the author's purpose in providing an explanation, describing a procedure, or discussing an experiment, and identify important issues that remain unresolved.
7. Integrate and evaluate multiple sources of information presented in diverse formats and media to address a question or solve a problem.
8. Evaluate the hypothesis, data, analysis, and conclusions in a science text, verifying the data when possible and corroborating or challenging conclusions with other information.
9. Synthesize information from a range of sources into a coherent understanding of a process, phenomenon, or concept, resolving conflicting information when possible.
10. By the end of grade twelve, read and comprehend science texts independently and proficiently.

Key Writing Standards

1. Introduce precise and knowledgeable claims. Establish the significance of the claims and distinguish them from alternate or opposing claims. Establish and maintain a formal style and objective tone. Provide a concluding statement that supports the argument presented.

2. Write informative text to examine and convey complex ideas. Develop topics thoroughly. Use precise language with appropriate and varied transitions and syntax. Provide a concluding statement.
3. Write narratives to describe events using effective technique, well-chosen details, and well-structured event sequences. Use precise words and phrases to convey a vivid picture of events.
4. Produce clear and coherent writing in which the development, organization, and style are appropriate to the task, purpose, and audience.
5. Develop and strengthen writing as needed by planning, revising, editing, rewriting, or trying a new approach, focusing on what is most significant for a specific purpose or audience.
6. Use technology, including the Internet, to produce, publish, and update individual and shared writing products.
7. Conduct short as well as sustained research projects to answer questions or solve problems.
8. Gather relevant information from multiple print and digital sources. Assess the strengths and limitations of various sources.
9. Draw evidence from informational texts to support analysis, reflection, and research.
10. Write routinely over extended and shorter time frames for a range of tasks, purposes, and audiences.

Key Speaking and Listening Standards

1. Initiate and participate effectively in collaborative discussions with diverse partners. Build on the ideas of others and express ideas clearly and persuasively.
2. Present information, findings, and supporting evidence to convey perspectives and logical arguments. Use appropriate eye contact, adequate volume, and clear pronunciation.
3. Make strategic use of digital media in presentations to enhance the understanding of findings.
4. Adapt speech to a variety of contexts and tasks, demonstrating a command of formal English.

Key Language Standards

1. Demonstrate command of standard English grammar and usage when writing and speaking.
2. Demonstrate command of standard English capitalization, punctuation, and spelling.

3. Acquire and use words and phrases sufficient for reading, writing, and speaking at the college- and career-readiness level.

COMMON CORE STATE STANDARDS: SOCIAL STUDIES

Key Reading Standards

1. Cite specific textual evidence to support the analysis of primary and secondary sources. Connect insights gained to an understanding of the text as a whole.
2. Determine the central ideas or information of a primary or secondary source. Provide an accurate summary that explains the relationships among key details and ideas.
3. Evaluate various explanations for actions or events, and determine which explanation best explains the textual evidence.
4. Determine the meanings of words and phrases as they are used in the text. Analyze how an author uses and refines the meanings of key terms over the course of a text.
5. Analyze in detail how a complex primary source is structured, including how key sentences, paragraphs, and larger portions contribute to the whole.
6. Evaluate the points of view of different authors on the same historical event or issue by assessing their claims, reasoning, and evidence.
7. Integrate and evaluate multiple sources of information presented in diverse formats and media to address a question or solve a problem.
8. Evaluate an author's premises, claims, and evidence by corroborating or challenging them with other information.
9. Integrate information from diverse sources, both primary and secondary, into a coherent understanding of an idea or event, noting discrepancies among sources.
10. By the end of grade twelve, read and comprehend history and social studies texts independently and proficiently.

Key Writing Standards

1. Introduce precise and knowledgeable claims. Establish the significance of the claims and distinguish them from alternate or opposing claims. Establish and maintain a formal style and objective tone. Provide a concluding statement that supports the argument presented.
2. Write informative text to examine and convey complex ideas. Develop topics thoroughly. Use precise language with appropriate and varied transitions and syntax. Provide a concluding statement.

3. Write narratives to describe events using effective technique, well-chosen details, and well-structured event sequences. Use precise words and phrases to convey a vivid picture of events.
4. Produce clear and coherent writing in which the development, organization, and style are appropriate to the task, purpose, and audience.
5. Develop and strengthen writing as needed by planning, revising, editing, rewriting, or trying a new approach, focusing on what is most significant for a specific purpose or audience.
6. Use technology, including the Internet, to produce, publish, and update individual and shared writing products.
7. Conduct short as well as sustained research projects to answer questions or solve problems.
8. Gather relevant information from multiple print and digital sources. Assess the strengths and limitations of various sources.
9. Draw evidence from informational texts to support analysis, reflection, and research.
10. Write routinely over extended and shorter time frames for a range of tasks, purposes, and audiences.

Key Speaking and Listening Standards

1. Initiate and participate effectively in collaborative discussions with diverse partners. Build on the ideas of others and express ideas clearly and persuasively.
2. Present information, findings, and supporting evidence to convey perspectives and logical arguments. Use appropriate eye contact, adequate volume, and clear pronunciation.
3. Make strategic use of digital media in presentations to enhance understanding and findings.
4. Adapt speech to a variety of contexts and tasks, demonstrating a command of formal English.

Key Language Standards

1. Demonstrate command of standard English grammar and usage when writing and speaking.
2. Demonstrate command of standard English capitalization, punctuation, and spelling.
3. Acquire and use words and phrases sufficient for reading, writing, and speaking at the college and career readiness level.

COMMON CORE STATE STANDARDS: ARTS, HEALTH, AND WORLD LANGUAGES

Key Reading Standards

1. Cite specific textual evidence to support the analysis of text, attending to important distinctions made by the author.
2. Determine the central ideas or conclusions of a text. Summarize complex concepts, processes, or information by paraphrasing in simpler but still accurate terms.
3. Follow complex, multistep procedures when performing technical tasks. Analyze results based upon explanations in the text.
4. Determine the meanings of symbols, key terms, and other domain-specific words and phrases as they are used in technical contexts.
5. Analyze how a text structures information or ideas into categories or hierarchies, demonstrating understanding of the information or ideas.
6. Analyze the author's purpose in providing an explanation, describing a procedure, or identifying important issues that remain unresolved.
7. Integrate and evaluate multiple sources of information presented in diverse formats and media to address a question or solve a problem.
8. Evaluate the hypothesis, data, analysis, and conclusions in a technical text, verifying the data when possible and corroborating or challenging conclusions with other information.
9. Synthesize information from a range of sources into a coherent understanding of a process, phenomenon, or concept, resolving conflicting information when possible.
10. By the end of grade twelve, read and comprehend a variety of texts independently and proficiently.

Key Writing Standards

1. Introduce precise and knowledgeable claims. Establish the significance of the claims and distinguish them from alternate or opposing claims. Establish and maintain a formal style and objective tone. Provide a concluding statement that supports the argument presented.
2. Write informative text to examine and convey complex ideas. Develop topics thoroughly. Use precise language with appropriate and varied transitions and syntax. Provide a concluding statement.
3. Write narratives to describe events using effective technique, well-chosen details, and well-structured event sequences. Use precise words and phrases to convey a vivid picture of events.

4. Produce clear and coherent writing in which the development, organization, and style are appropriate to the task, purpose, and audience.
5. Develop and strengthen writing as needed by planning, revising, editing, rewriting, or trying a new approach, focusing on what is most significant for a specific purpose or audience.
6. Use technology, including the Internet, to produce, publish, and update individual and shared writing products.
7. Conduct short as well as sustained research projects to answer questions or solve problems.
8. Gather relevant information from multiple print and digital sources. Assess the strengths and limitations of various sources.
9. Draw evidence from informational texts to support analysis, reflection, and research.
10. Write routinely over extended and shorter time frames for a range of tasks, purposes, and audiences.

Key Speaking and Listening Standards

1. Initiate and participate effectively in collaborative discussions with diverse partners. Build on the ideas of others and express ideas clearly and persuasively.
2. Present information, findings, and supporting evidence to convey perspectives and logical arguments. Use appropriate eye contact, adequate volume, and clear pronunciation.
3. Make strategic use of digital media in presentations to enhance the understanding and findings.
4. Adapt speech to a variety of contexts and tasks, demonstrating a command of formal English.

Key Language Standards

1. Demonstrate command of standard English grammar and usage when writing and speaking.
2. Demonstrate command of standard English capitalization, punctuation, and spelling.
3. Acquire and use words and phrases sufficient for reading, writing, and speaking at the college and career readiness level.

Chapter 26

A Model Lesson

The bell rang and the fourth period began. The principal used his key to enter through the back door of room X-12. It was a tenth-grade English class.

There were about thirty-five students. The principal found an empty chair at the back of the classroom and sat down. The following Common Core State Standards were posted on the front whiteboard:

1. *Analyze a complex set of ideas or sequence of events. Explain how specific individuals, ideas, or events interact or develop.*
2. *Produce clear and coherent writing in which the development, organization, and style are appropriate to the task, purpose, and audience.*

The teacher stood at the front of the room, in front of the whiteboard where the standards were posted. She pointed to the first standard.

"Everybody, please read the first standard to yourself," said the teacher. "I will then call on one of you to read the standard and state it in your own words."

The teacher waited twenty seconds. Then she selected a student at random.

"John," said the teacher. "Please read the first standard and state it in your own words."

John read the standard and stated it in his own words.

"That was a clear explanation," said the teacher.

"Think to yourself," said the teacher. "Why do you think that standard is important?"

The teacher waited twenty seconds and chose another student at random.

"Alice," said the teacher. "Why do you think that standard is important?

"It's important because you have to be able to understand what you are reading and really know it," said Alice. *"And you should be able to explain it to another person."*

"That's a clear and concise explanation," said the teacher. *She went back to the board and pointed to the standards.*

"Everybody, please look at the second standard," said the teacher. *"I will give you sixty seconds to read the second standard to yourself and think about it. You will then explain the standard to your elbow partner."*

"Melanie," said the teacher. *"Please restate the instructions to the entire class."*

Melanie restated the instructions.

The teacher walked again to the front of the classroom. *"Ready, go,"* said the teacher.

The students read the second standard to themselves. The teacher went around the classroom and listened as the students explained the standard to each other.

Sixty seconds passed. The teacher called upon another randomly selected student to explain the learning standard.

* * *

This was a model lesson. It was carefully planned and centered on the Common Core State Standards. In addition, there was frequent checking for understanding that engaged all the students and required them to understand the concepts being taught.

The standards chosen were part of a three-week unit centered on reading comprehension and analysis, as well as on expressing ideas clearly in writing.

The teacher spent a significant amount of time checking for understanding and having students share their ideas with each other. On the surface, it may seem like this takes an excessive amount of time. In reality, however, this checking for understanding actually saves a great deal of time. Because the students know they may be called upon at any time, they listen very carefully and participate fully. This high level of engagement by every student results in much greater learning.

Chapter 27

Section Review

Your goal should be for every student to learn at the highest levels and become fully prepared for college. There are no quick fixes. But through sustained efforts every day that are focused on classroom instruction, you will bring about high levels of student achievement. Implementation of the following basic elements will ensure high levels of instruction in every classroom:

1. Observe classroom instruction every day and meet with teachers to provide feedback. Your visits should be unannounced. This makes it possible for you to be confident that you are getting an accurate picture. If teaching is not up to standard, keep observing and providing feedback. If improvement does not occur, the teacher must be evaluated appropriately.
2. Work with teachers to ensure they are planning thoroughly and aligning instruction with the Common Core State Standards. It is essential that the standards being taught are posted prominently. The teacher should have the students read the standards and discuss their importance at the beginning of each class period.
3. Make sure that teachers are checking for understanding frequently. It is especially important that they call upon students who are randomly selected. This brings about high levels of engagement so that students master the concepts being taught. It also gives the teacher an accurate picture of mastery levels.

Everything you ask of teachers should be research based, not opinion based. If you are observing teachers frequently, if teachers are aligning their instruction with the Common Core Standards, and if teachers are checking for understanding by calling upon students who are randomly selected, you will see steady improvements.

There are no quick fixes. It is very important to be patient and realize that genuine improvements take time. By taking the right steps every day to support effective instruction, you will make steady progress and bring about significant improvements in student achievement.

SCHOOL OPERATIONS

Chapter 28

Cleaning Needed

It was July 6, the principal's first day on the campus. In the morning, he met the previous principal and some teachers. He also met some of the office staff. Later in the afternoon, he took a tour of the campus.

The tour was very upsetting. The lawns needed mowing, and they had not been edged in months. The flower beds were full of weeds. Shrubs were ragged and overgrown. Litter was everywhere. Trees were overgrown, and many of them had dead branches. The parking lot was full of weeds growing through cracks in the asphalt. Some of the weeds were waist high.

The buildings were also in bad shape. The hallways and stairways were dark because of numerous burned-out lights. The ceiling in the main building was braced by exposed wooden beams. It reminded the principal of the bracing in a mineshaft.

When the principal inspected the restrooms, he saw broken toilets and broken stalls. Soap dispensers were gone. Hand driers had been knocked off the walls.

When the principal inspected the classrooms, the floors looked like they had not been mopped in months. Graffiti was written on walls, floors, cabinets, and desks. Books were torn up and lying on floors. Many of the rooms had broken furniture.

The more the principal saw, the worse he felt. School would be starting in two months. One way or another, the school would have to be cleaned up.

The principal began meeting with the maintenance staff every day at 7:00 a.m. During these meetings, he gave them specific assignments for the day. In the evening, he checked what they had done and made a work plan for the following day. The campus began to look better.

One month later, an assistant principal came on board who was able to provide closer supervision of the maintenance and custodial staff.

The assistant principal met with them every day, assigned them to complete specific tasks, and recognized their achievements. The appearance of the campus continued to improve.

A plant manager was assigned in October. More and more improvements occurred, and the school began to look significantly better. The improvements in the physical plant created a school environment that had a positive effect on learning.

* * *

The first step in cleaning up a school is to determine the reason for it not being clean. If there is a lack of adequate staff, it is important that you meet with the plant manager to identify the priorities. Health and sanitation come first. The next priority is for the grounds and hallways to be kept clean.

If your school is in bad condition because of vandalism, you must determine the cause of the vandalism and correct it. You cannot have a clean school if students are ditching classes, wandering the campus, and writing graffiti on the walls.

If your school is not clean due to leadership that needs to improve, it is very important that you meet frequently with your plant manager to discuss strategies for improvement. You should assign priorities and deadlines in writing. It is also helpful to take before-and-after pictures to measure progress.

It is also necessary that you lead by example. When you bend down to pick up a piece of paper or pull a weed, you are not just improving the appearance of your school. You are showing that you care. And when others see that you care, they will care too.

Chapter 29

The Foundation of Your Entire School

It was 10:00 a.m. on the last Saturday in August. School would be starting on the following Wednesday. The principal had stayed up all night on the computer checking every student's class schedule. All of the schedules were complete. Ninety-three percent of the students had received their first choice of classes. Seven percent of the students had received an alternate choice.

All of the class sizes were balanced. There was nothing more to check. The principal felt wonderful as he began printing the class schedules. The school year was going to get off to a great start.

* * *

In most cases it is counterproductive to strive for perfection. But the master schedule is different. It is the foundation of your entire school, and it must be done properly. If your master schedule is strong, students will receive the correct classes, class sizes will be balanced, and the school year will get off to a good start.

If your master schedule is weak, students will get the wrong classes, many of the classes will be overcrowded, and the school year will get off to a terrible start.

An effective master schedule will be built around the needs of the students. It will include advanced placement courses for students who have been achieving at high levels. It will also include intervention courses for students who need extra help. Conference periods will be evenly distributed throughout the school day. Basic and advanced courses will be evenly distributed between veteran and newer teachers.

All of the effort that you put into creating a strong master schedule will be worth it. If you do not yet know how to create a master schedule, it is very important that you learn. Otherwise, when you delegate it, you will not know what to check for. Never forget that the master schedule is the foundation of your entire school.

Chapter 30

Tragedy

It was a Monday, the first day of summer school. Class schedules had been issued successfully, and the school had opened smoothly. It was 11:00 a.m. when the principal returned to his office from visiting classrooms. Just as he entered the office, the phone rang.

It was one of the counselors. "Can you come to my office right away?" she asked. "It's an emergency."

"What's it about?" the principal asked.

"I am with two parents," said the counselor. "Their son drowned during a field trip to the beach on Friday night. They want to know if the school can help pay for the funeral."

The principal rushed to the counselor's office. It was a scene he would never forget. The parents were sitting quietly in two chairs across from the counselor's desk. A young child who appeared to be their daughter was sitting in the mother's lap. The parents did not speak any English. The counselor translated.

The son had gone to a beach party with a school club on Friday evening. During the party, he had gone into the water with some of the other students. A big wave hit the son and knocked him down.

But he did not know how to swim.

There were no lifeguards at the beach because it was dark. Every time the son tried to stand up, another wave crashed over him and knocked him down. One of the students tried to grab the son's arm and pull him out of the water. But the waves were too powerful, and he couldn't grab hold of the son. Another student tried to help, but the undercurrent kept pulling the son down. The waves kept crashing and crashing, and the son drowned.

The parents did not have any money. They wanted to know if the school could help pay for the funeral expenses. They wanted to take the son back to Mexico to be buried.

The principal felt numb.

* * *

The field trip to the beach had not been approved. For safety reasons, the school district did not approve trips to sites where students might go into the water. On all trips that were approved, transportation had to be provided by school bus, never by private automobile. Everything was scrutinized very closely for safety.

When the teacher who was with the students was questioned, she said the trip had been the idea of the students. The teacher thought it would be nice to celebrate the school year with the students and provide a way for them to have fun.

The students got to the beach in their own cars just before dark. They started a campfire in one of the fire rings and began roasting marshmallows. The teacher told the students to stay with her near the campfire and not go near the water. But while there were almost 30 students, she was the only adult. It was a tragedy waiting to happen, and it did happen.

Do not let this tragedy happen to you. Be sure to evaluate all field trips very carefully for safety. There should be at least one adult for every ten students. Make sure there is transportation by school bus, not by private auto. Be sure that the field trip location is safe. Be sure there is an emergency plan in the event of an injury or accident. Try to think of everything that could go wrong.

When parents give approval for their child to go on a field trip, they assume that the school will take all necessary safety precautions. They trust that the school will protect their child.

Be sure that you have a clearly written policy on field trips explaining all requirements that teachers must follow. You cannot approve any field trip that may not be safe. If a teacher violates the policy, you must go forward with disciplinary action.

Chapter 31

Another Tragedy

It was 7:15 a.m. when the principal got the news. It was a ninth grader. He had been shot and killed the night before. The victim and suspects were possible gang members.

The principal closed the door to his office and sat quietly to collect his thoughts. He pictured the student being shot. He pictured the student's mother crying. He pictured the grief that many of the students and teachers would be facing when they got the news. He knew that he had to keep his head clear and implement a careful plan to guide the school through the tragedy.

First, the principal called the student's home. He spoke with the student's aunt, who confirmed that the student had indeed lost his life. Shots had been fired near their home, and he had been hit by the gunfire. The student was rushed to the hospital, but the hospital was unable to save his life.

The principal called on his radio for the administrators and school police officers to immediately meet with him in his office.

When the principal spoke to the officers, they told him they had heard about the shooting. They knew that the victim was a suspected gang member. But they had not known that the victim was a student at the school. The lead officer called their sergeant to request assistance because there would be gang tensions. Both officers went out onto the campus to supervise and try to get additional information.

The principal asked the assistant principal over counseling to activate the school's crisis team and set up grief counseling in the library. The principal also asked her to call the district office and request additional crisis counselors.

The principal asked the assistant principal over instruction to assist with the logistics of setting up the crisis counseling. The principal also asked her to write a statement with general information that could be shared with any parents or members of public who called the school.

The principal asked the assistant principal over discipline to alert the deans and campus supervisors to be on high alert and to activate the emergency supervision team during nutrition, lunch, and after school. They needed to be alert for students who were experiencing grief, and to send them to the library for crisis counseling. They also needed to be alert for any signs of gang activity.

The principal asked the assistant principal over student services to print the class schedule of the victim and meet immediately with the first-period teacher. The principal would be making a public address announcement during period one, and he wanted the teacher to know about the situation ahead of time.

At 7:45 a.m., the principal called the district office to inform his supervisor. The principal then started writing his statement for the public address announcement.

At 8:30 a.m., the principal made a public address announcement to the entire school to explain the tragedy.

"Good morning," said the principal. "I have an important announcement for all students and staff members. I regret to report that one of our students (name withheld), a ninth grader, has lost his life. There was an incident yesterday near his home in which shots were fired. I regret to say that he lost his life as a result of being struck by gunfire. Could we please have a moment of silence in his memory?"

"(Name withheld) was an important member of our school family," said the principal. "I know that he was a friend to many of you. As you go through the day today, please think about the good memories that you have of him. Teachers, we will have grief counseling in the library on an as-needed basis. If you feel that a student is in need of this, please write a hall pass and send the student to the library.

"We will be placing our flag at half-staff for the next three days in recognition of (name withheld)," said the principal. "We will conduct a school fundraiser to help his family beginning tomorrow. Please remember (name withheld) as you go through your day today. Please think about his family, and please provide any support you can for those who were closest to him. This concludes my announcement. Thank you."

The principal spent the rest of the day going to each of the deceased student's classes to talk to his classmates. Each class received two blank sympathy cards for the students to express their condolences. The principal also spent time in the library, where the counselors provided grief counseling.

The school went on high alert to prevent gang activity during passing periods, nutrition, and lunch. School police officers provided extra patrols in the neighborhood after school. Fortunately, there were no incidents.

A fundraiser implemented on the following day brought in over $600.00. The principal went to the home of the deceased student and presented the money to his mother on the evening before the funeral.

* * *

When a student or faculty member dies, it can quickly turn your school upside down. It is very important that you have a plan in place ahead of time. Do your best to think of everything that needs to be done. Try hard to think of everything you can do to make the situation easier.

It is a good idea to have a crisis box with items such as blank sympathy cards, letter paper for students to write notes to family members, and instructions for crisis counselors. Teachers should be provided with instructions for handling students who are grieving. You should also have a plan for sending grieving students home if they are unable to continue through the school day.

You must also have a strong emergency supervision plan. If the death is gang related, additional staff should be placed on duty during passing periods, lunch, and after school to prevent gang activity. It is very important that you check restrooms for any new graffiti that might appear. It is also very important that you have a network of confidential student informants who will let you know of potential problems.

Chapter 32

Almost a Disaster

It was 9:00 p.m., the third Saturday of August. The principal was working in his office. Everyone else was gone. School was scheduled to start in twelve days.

They had been planning for almost an entire year to divide the school of 3,500 students into seven small learning communities. Each learning community was to have five hundred students. Teachers had been selected, they had a strong organization plan, and everything was ready on paper.

The master schedule had been divided into seven sections, one for each small learning community. Unfortunately, no matter what he did, the principal could not get the class sizes to balance. In addition, he could not get the computer to schedule students into all of the classes they needed.

There was nothing he could do to make the master schedule work unless he increased the number of separate subjects that each teacher would teach. But he had told the teachers during the previous spring that he would not do that.

The phone rang. It was his wife.

"How's it going?" she asked.

"I am just so frustrated," said the principal. "I can't get this master schedule together."

"Has it gotten any better since this morning?" she asked.

"No. Nothing I do works," said the principal. "I have done all kinds of changes, and all kinds of adjustments. But I cannot get it to work."

"Is it still because of the small learning communities?" she asked.

"That's exactly the reason," said the principal. "It's the same problem I have been having all week. At this point, the computer is only scheduling seventy-three percent of the students into all of the classes they need. And when it does, the class sizes are way out of balance. There will be forty-five kids in one English class, and fifteen kids in another."

"Would it help to come home and start on it fresh in the morning?" she asked.

"It's deeper than that," said the principal. "The only way I can fix the master schedule is to give each teacher three to four separate classes to teach. And I can't do that."

"How much longer do you think you will be?" she asked.

"I'm not sure," said the principal. "I will call you before I leave."

They ended the call, and the principal kept working. When he left to go home at 11:30 p.m., it was still not any better.

When he woke up in the morning, the principal made the decision not to implement small learning communities. This meant converting the master schedule from seven smaller units back into one big unit for the entire school. He did not finish the master schedule until three days before school began. It was almost a disaster.

* * *

The master schedule is a period-by-period list of every class that is taught and every teacher who teaches those classes. It is the foundation for programming students into the classes they need. If you set it up properly, the computer will automatically schedule students into the proper classes and class sizes will be balanced. If you do not set it up properly, classes will not be balanced, many students will get the wrong classes, and you will have to change hundreds of class schedules after the school year begins.

You should never jeopardize your school by experimenting on a large scale with the master schedule. If something goes wrong, you will have a terrible problem that you cannot correct and which will seriously hurt your school.

Chapter 33

Phone Calls

It was the third week of July. The principal was attending a district meeting for high school principals. It was 11:30 a.m., and the assistant superintendent over high schools was finishing his remarks.

"There is one last thing," said the assistant superintendent. "It is essential that you return every phone call as soon as possible, and within 24 hours at the latest. Don't ever let me get a complaint that you have not returned a phone call promptly."

* * *

Whenever somebody calls you, it's important. There might be an important need. There might be a serious problem. Or there might be an important question.

When you call back right away, you are showing respect and courtesy. If the other person is calling with a complaint, you have already taken a positive step to resolve the complaint.

If the other person is calling with a question or some other important need, you are also being helpful when you call back right away. Being helpful is a two-way street. When you are helpful to other people, most of the time they are going to be helpful back to you. The quicker you return phone calls to others, the quicker others will return phone calls to you. This is a very important part of being a professional.

Returning phone calls promptly will make your job much easier and help your career. You will solve problems quicker, you will earn the respect of others, and others will help you more. Failing to return phone calls promptly will make your job more difficult and jeopardize your career. Your perceived lack of professionalism will eventually come back to haunt you.

Chapter 34

The Entire Contract

It was a meeting for district principals, and they were coming to the last item on the agenda before the break. The principal was looking forward to the break because that's where he always got the most benefit. He usually learned a lot from talking with the other principals. He also needed to stand up and stretch his legs.

The next person on the agenda was a district administrator talking about the union contract. He was describing a situation at one of the schools where there had been a problem.

"And don't ever think that it is okay to grant exceptions to any part of the teachers' contract," said the administrator. "If you do, you will cause all kinds of problems for yourself."

"Here is an example," said the administrator. "Suppose you have a teacher with a child care problem who is asking for a first-period conference so she can arrive to school late, at 8:00 a.m. instead of 7:50 a.m. You would like to grant her the exception, because she is a dedicated teacher who does a great job for kids."

"But you just cannot do it," said the administrator. "First of all, the teachers' contract is school district policy, and you do not have the authority to change district policy. Second, if you ever did grant an exception, you could be grieved if another teacher wanted the same exception and you said no. Third, you could be accused of being unfair because of following other areas of the contract that you did feel were necessary. You do not get to pick and choose. You have to follow the entire contract."

* * *

You cannot be an effective principal unless you have the respect of your teachers. And if you are not respecting your teachers' contract, you are going to cause big problems for yourself.

First of all, if it's in the union contract, it's also an official policy of your school district. That means that you will get yourself in trouble with your supervisor if you do not follow the contract.

Next, if it's in the union contract, it's an item that has already been thoroughly negotiated. The teacher's contract is what they agreed to. You do not have the right to dishonor those negotiations by granting exceptions.

Finally, and most important, it's an integrity issue. If you are granting exceptions to the contract by looking the other way, it's a form of lying. And if teachers think you are being dishonest in any way, they are going to lose respect for you.

Some people believe that it is better to seek forgiveness than to ask permission. In other words, they think that it's okay to play games, tell white lies, and do things they know are wrong.

Don't ever go down that road. People do not respect you if they cannot believe you. Sometimes you can get away with playing games and acting like you didn't know any better. But eventually it will catch up with you. And once it does, your career and your reputation will be permanently damaged.

Chapter 35

The Right Kind of Faculty Meeting

It was 2:45 p.m. when the principal got to the multipurpose room. The tables and chairs, enough for 180 people, were ready to go. He checked the microphone and connected his laptop to the LCD projector. He then set out the agendas, the sign-in rosters, and the stickers for name badges.

The teachers started coming in at about 3:10 p.m. It always amazed the principal to see the multipurpose room fill up with teachers. There were so many of them. He started the meeting at 3:20 p.m.

* * *

When the principal got to the meeting room, it was 6:45 a.m. There were five tables with six chairs per table, enough for thirty people. He set out the agendas, sign-in sheets, and name badges. He also set up his computer and the LCD projector.

The teachers started coming in at 7:00 a.m. In addition to this meeting before school, there would be meetings during periods two, four, and six. Tomorrow there would be meetings during periods one, three, five, and after school.

During the meetings, he would be asking teachers for their ideas on building positive student attitudes. He always looked forward to these meetings, because the teachers really got to talk and be involved.

* * *

A big part of leadership is communication. And the setting you choose for communication is very important.

In some cases, it is best if you speak to large groups, even if you have 150 to two hundred teachers. This is appropriate if you have a simple message, or if everybody on your staff needs to hear the same thing at the same time. A big setting is great for celebrations. It is also appropriate when you need to promote faculty unity.

In other cases, it is much better if you speak to small groups. This makes it possible for you to have discussions, with two-way communication instead of one-way communication. It gives you a much better feeling for your teachers. It also gives your teachers a much better feeling for you.

Think about what you are trying to accomplish when you plan the setting for a faculty meeting. If you need to promote faculty unity and your message is basic, large faculty meetings are very appropriate. If you need discussions with small groups of teachers or if your message is detailed, period-by-period faculty meetings are best.

Chapter 36

Section Review

You cannot have effective instruction unless you have effective school operations. The following elements will help you in creating effective school operations:

1. Make sure that you have the strongest possible master schedule. Be sure that classes are balanced ahead of time, and that every student is scheduled properly.
2. Provide teachers with the textbooks, instructional materials, and equipment they need.
3. Make sure that you have clean and well-maintained classrooms, buildings, and landscaping.
4. Read your teachers' contract and know it thoroughly.
5. Make sure that you scrutinize field trips very carefully.
6. Have plans in place for special needs, such as grief counseling and gang prevention.

LEADERSHIP

Chapter 37

Delegation

It was 8:00 p.m. The principal was sitting in his office doing paperwork. The portable room heater was set on maximum. But it was still cold, and the principal was wearing his sweatshirt.

When his wife called at 8:30 p.m., the principal told her that he would be leaving to come home in about twenty minutes.

When his wife called again at 9:30 p.m., the principal told her that he was wrapping up.

When the principal left to drive home at 10:30 p.m., he realized that he had been working on a job that one of the assistant principals should have been doing.

* * *

To be an effective leader, you must learn how to multiply yourself so that everybody in your organization is working effectively. This means that you must learn how to delegate.

If you do not learn how to delegate, you will seriously limit the effectiveness of your school. You will cause yourself to get bogged down in details that will take away your ability to see the big picture. And you cannot be an effective leader if you lose sight of the big picture.

Delegation does not mean dumping the job on somebody and hoping for the best. You must carefully plan the jobs that you delegate. You must provide written deadlines. You must also check early on implementation to ensure that progress is being made.

It is very important to delegate the entire job, not just parts of the job. For example, many high schools have an athletics director who reports to an assistant principal. This means that you, as the principal, should never bypass the assistant principal and go directly to the athletics director with instructions. If you do, you will soon find that your athletics director is coming to you for direction when he should be going to the assistant principal.

You must also have an effective way to record the tasks you have delegated. One way of doing this is to use an Excel spreadsheet. Create one column that describes the job, one column with the name of the person assigned to the job, and one column with the due date. Look at the spreadsheet frequently and keep it updated. Another effective way to record delegated tasks is to write them on a whiteboard in your office. This makes it easy for people to see all of the tasks that have been assigned.

You must not fall into the trap of trying to do everything yourself. If you do, you will find yourself unable to provide effective leadership because you are drowning in details. The better you learn to delegate, the more effective you will be as a principal.

Chapter 38

Delegation Gone Bad

It was 11:30 a.m. When the principal got back to his office, he was so upset. All he could do was stare out the window in frustration. He had delegated a job to one of the assistant principals, and there had been numerous mistakes. It was now a serious problem.

Later in the day, the principal thought about it more. He realized that much of the problem had been his fault. He should have done a better job of delegation.

* * *

You need diversity to have a strong management team. That means having a variety of different working styles, and a variety of different skills. It also means that you need to use different management styles for the different people on your administrative team.

Some people function best with management that is highly structured. These people work hard. But they need guidance from you that is structured, especially if they are doing something for the first time. They need written procedures and deadlines. They also need to know that you are going to check on them to see that the work is done right. If these things are provided, they will function at very high levels.

Other people function best with a less directive style of management. These people are often highly creative, and they like to figure things out for themselves. You need to be close to these people and know what they are doing. You also need to provide encouragement. But you can't be too directive or too structured. If you are, you will destroy their spirit and make them very unhappy. You will also inhibit the creativity that is needed to make your school better.

The basic solution is to know your people very well and provide the management style that is right for them as individuals.

You also need to have open communication with your people. They have to know that you are going to listen to them and be patient with them. They have to know that they can come to you if they are falling behind or having trouble. They must also know that you are going to support their efforts to do a good job.

Finally, the people on your administrative team must know that they have to do a good job and produce positive results. This means that you must evaluate them honestly and hold them accountable if they are not doing an effective job. It is never fun to do progressive discipline or give a below-standard evaluation. But you must never back down from this responsibility. If you do, you will be hurting your school.

Chapter 39

Deadlines

It was 9:30 a.m. on Thursday. The principal had just gotten back to his office when one of the assistant principals came to his door.

"I'm sorry," said the assistant principal. "I know this project is due to the district office tomorrow. But I just don't think that I can get it done."

The principal looked on his delegation list and saw that he had given her the project a month ago. He had also talked to her about it last week, and she had told him that things were going fine.

"Today is Thursday, and the project is due tomorrow," said the principal. "Why are you telling me this now?"

"I'm really sorry," said the assistant principal. "I know I should have started it sooner."

"When did I give you the project?" asked the principal.

"Last month," said the assistant principal.

"When did you start working on the project?" asked the principal.

"I started it on Monday," said the assistant principal.

"How many hours do you think the project will take?" asked the principal.

"I'm not sure," said the assistant principal.

"How much time have you spent on the project so far?" asked the principal.

"About three hours," said the assistant principal.

"Are you saying that I should do the project for you, and the deadline is tomorrow?" asked the principal.

The assistant principal didn't say anything.

"I know that you have a lot of things going on. But I need you to close your door, focus, and get this done," said the principal. "Don't let anything interrupt you except lunch supervision. Put everything else on hold. There is nothing more important for you at this time than this project. I need you to

bring me the draft by 6:00 tonight. I will then go over it with you to see if any changes are needed."

"But I have church tonight," said the assistant principal.

"You have to get this done," said the principal.

The draft was completed at 6:30 p.m. The principal went over it with her, and it was pretty good. The assistant principal made the changes that were needed and the final draft was completed by 7:00 p.m. The assistant principal met all future deadlines.

* * *

There will always be too much going on. And there will always be too much work to do. But you cannot teach kids with excuses. And you will not improve your school by letting the people on your administrative team make excuses.

You must put a deadline on every assignment that you give to your administrators. You should put their assignments in writing. You should also go to your administrators early to check on their progress.

It takes a lot of time. It can also be uncomfortable. But in the long run you will gain time and multiply your effectiveness.

Always remember that you will get blamed for everything at your school that goes wrong.

The people on your staff simply must get their jobs done. If they are not producing and you do not correct the problem, you are jeopardizing your school.

You are also jeopardizing your career.

Chapter 40

Ask Questions

It was a meeting of the department chairpersons. They were talking about how to improve student achievement.

One of the department chairs spoke up: "I heard about a great program from a friend of mine in another school district. They took the lowest-achieving kids and created a special program just for them. They call it the Opportunity Academy. The kids are housed in a far corner of the campus, and they are isolated from the rest of the school. It keeps the bad kids from ruining it for the good kids."

"What happened to the achievement of the kids in the academy?" the principal asked.

"I don't know," said the department chair.

"How do the kids feel about being in the academy?" the principal asked.

"I don't know," said the department chair.

"How do their parents feel?" the principal asked.

"I am not sure," said the department chair.

The idea died, and they went on to the next topic. The meeting ended about thirty minutes later.

If the principal had told the department chair that he disagreed with her because isolating low-achieving students was a form of discrimination, it would have put her on the spot and made her feel that she had to defend the idea. It might have also created a dynamic in which her colleagues felt that they had to defend the idea.

But by asking the right questions, the principal was able to express disagreement without causing the department chair to feel defensive. This kept a bad idea from taking root. It also showed the others at the meeting how to disagree in a respectful way without getting personal.

* * *

Most educators are nice people. They don't like to argue. They also like to have positive relationships with their colleagues. So when a bad idea comes up in a meeting and they don't know how to object to the idea in a nice way, they often say nothing. Suddenly a bad idea takes root because people who know better have remained silent.

If you ask the right questions, you can object to just about anything in a nice way. First, it does not cause the person who is proposing the idea to feel like he or she is being put down. Second, it keeps people focused on goals. Third, it prevents arguments and keeps the discussion moving in a positive direction.

Chapter 41

A Sacrifice You Must Make

It was a Thursday after school. The principal was standing at the gas station on the corner. An assistant principal was standing next to him. The sheriff's deputy assigned to the school was standing about twenty feet away, next to his police car. The chief safety officer was with him. There had been a rumor of possible gang activity after school. So far, it was quiet. The kids seemed pretty normal.

"Did you hear about the TGIF tomorrow?" the assistant principal asked.

"I heard about it," said the principal. "But I don't go to those things. I used to go all the time when I was in the classroom. But it's not a good idea when you are an administrator."

They continued watching the students. Some of the students were crossing the street going north. Some of them were crossing east toward a small shopping center.

"Why not?" the assistant principal asked.

"When you go to those things you can get yourself into some very awkward situations," said the principal. "First, there is drinking involved, and it doesn't help your career to have gossip going around that you are a drinker."

As the principal looked toward the shopping center, it seemed like there were more kids than usual over there. "You can also get yourself into situations where there are conflicts involving social relationships and work relationships," said the principal.

"What do you mean?" the assistant principal asked.

Suddenly it was happening. About fifteen kids started grouping across the street at the shopping center. There was going to be a fight. The principal got on the radio. "Code G, shopping center!"

The principal and the assistant principal quickly crossed the street against the red light and started walking toward the trouble. When the students *started fighting, the principal and the assistant principal began running. The deputy and the safety officer were following right behind them in the police car.*

* * *

Your job is your job, and you should keep it that way. If you start confusing professional relationships and social relationships, you are going to cause big problems for yourself. You will jeopardize your ability to make hard decisions. You will also jeopardize your ability to lead.

Suppose you are a new principal, and you decide to socialize with a group of teachers after school on a Friday, with happy hour and drinks. You stay late, you enjoy yourself, and you get to know some teachers on a social level.

Two weeks later, you get a complaint from a parent about one of the teachers with whom you were socializing. According to the parent, the teacher is ineffective and makes abusive remarks to the students. Because of the social relationship you have formed with the teacher, you are now in a difficult position for implementing employee discipline or giving a below-standard evaluation.

Or suppose you have to make a difficult decision regarding the master schedule. Due to the needs of students, you make a decision that favors a math teacher over an art teacher. However, because you have had a social relationship with the math teacher, the perception by many is that you decided in favor of the math teacher because you know that teacher socially.

You have now placed yourself in a situation where people are questioning your judgment and they think you are showing favoritism. You have jeopardized your credibility and your ability to lead.

When you are a leader, you must keep the relationships with your coworkers balanced. You need to be friendly and accessible. But you should not cross the line by developing social relationships. Failing to keep a balance will jeopardize your effectiveness, your school, and your career.

Chapter 42

Priorities

It was a Saturday morning in November. The principal was working alone in his office. It was still his first year. An improved discipline policy was now in place and it was working. And they had stabilized the master schedule.

The feeling the principal got from the teachers was that they were glad about the improvements that had been made. But he also got a feeling for how bad things had been. The school had been in serious turmoil. There had been a history of major disruptions and chaos going back fifteen years.

His goal for the day was to start going through the files in his office. When he had first moved in, all of the file cabinets had been packed full. In addition, many files had been placed in cardboard boxes stacked in his closet. His plan was to look at the files and throw away anything that didn't need to be saved.

As he went through the files, the principal felt like he was going back in time. A lot of them could be thrown away. But some of them had to be saved.

One of the things he noticed was a box full of parent/student handbooks. The handbooks were about fifty pages long and printed in color on glossy paper. All of the school policies were explained, and there was a detailed calendar listing school activities for the entire year. They were beautiful. The principal had been at a lot of schools. These were the best handbooks he had ever seen.

He also found files with reports describing major incidents at the school. There were detailed write-ups on fights, parent complaints, and conflicts between staff members. Some of the reports even described conflicts between administrators. It was disturbing to read the reports because of the problems they described. But it was interesting to the principal that they were all typed, well written, and very professional.

Instead of working with students, supporting teachers, and making the school better, it appeared that the previous administrators had spent most *of their time sitting in their offices, writing reports, and creating fancy handbooks.*

* * *

You cannot improve a school if the administrators are spending an excessive amount of time in their offices. They should be out on the campus and inside classrooms, working with students and supporting teachers. They should be so busy doing real work that they don't have time to spend time on handbooks and reports that do little to improve learning.

Chapter 43

Also Listen to the Quiet Voices

"I have been teaching here for thirty-five years," said the teacher. "I know these kids. And I guarantee they will not read!"

It was after school. The principal was meeting with a group of department chairs in the faculty lounge. The room was hot because the sun was beating in. They could not keep the sun out because the blinds were broken.

They were discussing the possibility of implementing a sustained silent reading program. Reading scores had been very low, and improving reading was the most urgent need. The principal was asking the department chairs for their input. He was writing their comments on chart paper.

"Do you really think your kids will not read?" the principal asked.

"Trust me," said the teacher. "I know what I am talking about. These kids are not going to read. They are just going to play around."

The principal wrote those comments on the chart paper.

"We had sustained silent reading when I taught middle school," said the chairperson of the Science Department. "I have seen this work. The key is to get materials that the kids will want to read."

There was a pause as the principal wrote those comments on the chart paper.

"I think you are right," said the chairperson of the English Department. "I believe the kids will read if we get interesting reading material."

"I agree," said the chairperson of the Special Education Department. "When I was in college, we read a book called Hooked on Books. It describes how they improved reading scores for kids in reform schools by providing high-interest paperbacks for them to read."

At the conclusion of the meeting, there was an agreement that they would implement sustained silent reading. The next step was to determine when they would schedule the sustained silent reading period.

Six weeks later, they implemented sustained silent reading. The department chair who had voiced the strongest opposition to the plan eventually became one of its strongest advocates.

* * *

You will not improve your school unless you make changes. But you cannot move forward unless you make the right changes. You must look at the research, get people involved, and plan carefully.

It is crucial that you listen to all of the voices when you are developing plans to improve your school. You need the participation of parents, students, and teachers. You must listen to everybody who will have to carry out the plan. You must also listen to everybody who will be affected by the plan.

It is important to remember that the loudest voices are not always the wisest voices. You must also listen carefully to the quiet voices. You will not improve your school if you let the loud voices drown out the wise voices.

Chapter 44

We Are Not As Bad As . . .

It was their weekly administrative staff meeting. They were looking at a list of high schools and their most recent test scores.

One of the assistant principals spoke up. "Look at this," she said. "We are not on the bottom anymore. In fact, we are doing better than a lot of schools. We should be proud!"

"It's nice to be off the bottom," said the principal. "But the most important thing is that we have been going up every year," he said. "That's what really counts."

"But at least we are not on the bottom anymore," said the assistant principal.

"That's true," said the principal. "But think of it this way. Unless you are on the very bottom, there will always be at least one other school that is worse than you. It doesn't mean that you are doing a good job just because you are better than a lot of other bad schools."

* * *

You should never think that you are doing a good job just because another school is doing worse. There will always be another school that is worse. Your focus should be on continuous improvement for your school. That is the mark of real success.

Chapter 45

Making People Happy Is Not Your Job

It was September 8, and school would be opening on the following day. The faculty meeting was over. The principal was walking back to the main building with one of the teachers.

"How long have you been a principal?" the teacher asked.

"Eleven years," said the principal. "The time has gone by so fast."

"Do you ever feel that no matter what you decide, you just can't win?" the teacher asked.

"I don't feel that way," said the principal. "But I do have to make decisions that will make some people unhappy."

"How do you deal with it?" the teacher asked.

"I have to keep reminding myself that I am not here to make people happy," said the principal. "We are only here to help these kids learn."

* * *

Sometimes as a principal you will get to make easy decisions. Most of the time, however, you will have to make the hard ones. When it is a difficult decision, no matter what you decide, some people are going to be unhappy.

When you find yourself in that position, do your best to keep your mind clear and think about what is best for the students. That will keep you going in the right direction.

Another thing that will help you is getting people who disagree to meet together and talk about all sides of the issue. This creates a setting where all sides of the issue get discussed. When the decision is made and some people do not agree, at least they have had a chance to explain their side of the issue. And at least they have heard the other side.

Sometimes parents will want you to make decisions that benefit their own kids while being detrimental to other kids. In a situation like that, it is important to make a statement before the discussion starts that the members of the group should only be discussing proposals that are good for all students.

It will also help you to make better decisions if you slow down and ask yourself the following questions:

1. What are the advantages and disadvantages?
2. Is the decision based upon reliable information?
3. Will the decision preserve the safety of students and staff?
4. Is the decision educationally sound?
5. Can the decision be implemented well by everyone involved?
6. Is it honest and open?
7. How much time and money will it cost to implement the decision?
8. Does the decision follow the contract and district guidelines?
9. Have those who will be affected by the decision had meaningful input?

You must do your best to make wise decisions and keep your sights on the needs of students. You must also focus on the needs of your staff and the resources they need. It is not about making people happy. It is about making decisions that will help to improve learning.

Chapter 46

He Went Over to His Shelf

It was December. The principal was sitting in his office with a new teacher. She had gotten off to a rough start. The kids were giving her a very hard time, and it was starting to affect her physically. The teacher had been sick four times already. She had also been late to school six times.

"I feel overwhelmed," said the teacher. "I get home at night, and I am exhausted. All I do is work. When I try to check papers and complete my lesson plans, I fall asleep. Twice a week I go to night school to finish the requirements for my teaching credential. I don't think I can take it anymore."

The teacher started to cry. The principal got up to get her some tissue.

"Vacation is coming up," said the principal. "That will give you some time to get rested. Did you know that you are going through the same thing that most new teachers go through?"

"Are you kidding?" said the teacher. "I thought it was just me."

"It was the same thing for me when I started out. And it happens a lot," said the principal. "Has your instructional coach been working with you?"

"He has come to my classroom about five times," said the teacher. "We have been meeting together during my conference period. He has given me some good ideas."

"Try to understand that things will start getting better for you," said the principal. "Based upon my visits to your classroom, you are doing much better than you think."

The principal went over to his shelf where he had a number of books on effective teaching. "This first book is The First Days of School, *by Harry and Rosemary Wong,*" said the principal. "It's one of the best books I have seen on classroom teaching,"

He then found a second book. "And this one is Assertive Discipline, *by Lee and Marlene Canter," he said. "It's a great book on establishing classroom discipline."*

The principal gave her both books. "If you read these books over vacation, I think they will help you," said the principal.

"I'm sorry for coming in here and losing it," said the teacher.

"That's okay," said the principal. "I will talk to your instructional coach and ask him to stop by your classroom more often. Make sure that you really talk to him and let him know how things are going for you."

The teacher seemed to feel better when she left the principal's office. The principal hoped that she would be able to feel better about the job she was doing.

* * *

When you keep books on teaching and educational leadership in your office, it makes it easy for you to lend the books out so that others may also learn from them. The following books will be helpful to you and others:

1. *A Place Called School*, by John Goodlad, is a classic study on schooling and reforms to improve education in the United States.
2. *Always Running*, by Louis Rodriguez, describes the experiences of a young gang member and the events that nearly destroyed his life.
3. *Assertive Discipline*, by Lee and Marlene Canter, describes effective practices to improve classroom discipline and reduce disruptions.
4. *Classroom Instruction that Works*, by Robert Marzano, Debra Pickering, and Jane Pollock, describes research-based classroom practices that improve student achievement.
5. *Change or Die*, by Alan Deutschman, discusses human behavior and provides suggestions for helping people break bad habits and bring about positive changes in their lives.
6. *Explicit Direct Instruction,* by John Hollingsworth and Silvia Ybarra, explains classroom strategies for implementing effective, standards-based instructions.
7. *Fires in the Bathroom*, by Kathleen Cushman, provides advice for teachers from students on humanizing the education process.
8. *Focus*, by Mike Schmoker, provides advice for implementing strategies that improve teaching, with a strong emphasis on improving literacy.
9. *Good to Great*, by Jim Collins, is a classic study on effective leadership and the practices that bring about success in large organizations.
10. *Hooked on Books*, by Daniel Fader and Elton McNeil, describes successful efforts to improve reading skills by providing students with interesting reading materials.

11. *Horace's Compromise,* by Theodore Sizer, examines American high schools and provides solutions for increasing personalization.
12. *How to Get Your Point Across in 30 Seconds or Less,* by Milo Frank, describes effective communication strategies that move people to action.
13. *Influencer,* by Kerry Patterson, Joseph Grenny, David Maxfield, Ron McMillan, and Al Switzler, explains strategies for getting people to make positive changes in their lives.
14. *In Search of Excellence,* by Tom Peters and Robert Waterman, is a classic study on the leadership strategies that create effective organizations.
15. *Inside the Crips,* by Colton Simpson, describes the life of a gang member and the culture of violence in gangs.
16. *Leadership for Low-Performing Schools,* by Daniel Duke, is a practical, step-by-step guide on the process for implementing school turnarounds.
17. *Learning by Doing,* by Richard DuFour, Rebecca DuFour, Robert Eaker, and Thomas Many, focuses on the people skills needed to implement professional learning communities.
18. *Life's Greatest Lessons,* by Hal Urban, provides advice to young people on achieving success in their lives.
19. *Making the Corps,* by Thomas E. Ricks, describes the experiences of U.S. Marines in basic training and the strategies that bring about confident, positive attitudes in young people.
20. *Professional Learning Communities at Work,* by Richard DuFour and Robert Eaker, describes strategies to improve teaching by creating professional learning communities.
21. *Results,* by Mike Schmoker, provides examples of proven strategies to improve schools and raise student achievement.
22. *Successful School Change,* by Claude Goldenberg, describes efforts taken to bring about change at an urban elementary school that significantly improved student achievement.
23. *The First Days of School,* by Harry and Rosemary Wong, is an outstanding guide for all teachers on providing effective instruction.
24. *The Seven Habits of Highly Effective Teens,* by Sean Covey, is an excellent resource to help students achieve success in their lives.
25. *The Slight Edge,* by Jeff Olson, is a self-improvement guide that emphasizes the power of setting goals and working toward them by taking small steps every day.
26. *There Are No Shortcuts,* by Rafe Esquith, describes the successful efforts of a teacher at an urban elementary school in Los Angeles.
27. *Turnaround,* by William Bratton, describes the successful efforts of the New York City Police Commissioner to significantly reduce street crime.
28. *Switch,* by Chip and Dan Heath, discusses the basic elements that help people develop positive habits and mindsets.

29. *Up the Organization*, by Robert Townsend, describes successful strategies for improving organizations by reducing bureaucracy.
30. *What Great Principals Do Differently*, by Todd Whitaker, focuses on leadership and people skills for principals. It is written by a former principal.
31. *What Great Teachers Do Differently*, by Todd Whitaker, focuses on positive practices that bring about high levels of student achievement.
32. *What Works in Schools*, by Robert Marzano, explains research-based strategies that bring about significant improvements in student achievement.
33. *You Haven't Taught Until They Have Learned*, by Swen Nater and Ronald Gallimore, describes the teaching practices of legendary basketball coach John Wooden.

Chapter 47

Pick Up the Phone

It was 4:00 p.m. when she walked into the principal's office. It was the assistant principal who was responsible for staff development. She did not have a happy look on her face.

"I have the schedule of staff development for the whole year all mapped out," said the assistant principal.

The principal looked at the schedule carefully and frowned. "Not much room left for teacher collaboration," said the principal. "That is what we need more than anything else."

"I know," said the assistant principal. "But this is the best I could do with all of the requirements from the district office that we have to fit in."

The staff development requirements from the district were not what was best for the school. When the assistant principal left his office, the principal picked up his phone and called the district office.

* * *

It is a fact of life that you must follow orders if you want to keep your job. But it is also a fact of life that your supervisor will not always know what is best for your school. If your district office is asking you to do something that you do not believe in, it is essential that you contact your supervisor to respectfully suggest something different.

Every time you speak up in a responsible and respectful manner, even if you do not agree with your supervisor, you are demonstrating that you are a leader who thinks carefully about the welfare of your school.

If you do not speak up when there is a bad idea, you are risking the welfare and future of your students. You are also risking your career.

If a bad idea goes wrong, even if it comes from the district office, it will be you who gets the blame, not the district office.

Chapter 48

A Leader Who Got Things Done

School was going to start in six days. The principal was walking around the campus with the superintendent. They came to an area by the gym where all of the grass had died.

"What's going on with this grass?" the superintendent asked.

"The pipes for the sprinkler system got busted during the construction," said the principal. "There was no water here for about three months."

"Are the pipes fixed now?" the superintendent asked.

"They got fixed last week," said the principal.

The superintendent walked over to side, out of the principal's earshot, and got on his cell phone. He appeared to be upset.

After about a minute, the superintendent finished the call and came back to the principal. "I just made arrangements for sod to be put in," he said.

They continued their tour of the campus. Three days later a crew arrived to install sod.

* * *

This was a leader who fixed a major problem with a one-minute phone call. What was it about his leadership that made that happen?

First, above all else, he cared about the students. He wanted all of the students to go to effective schools. He was driven to create better schools.

Next, he was honest if he didn't like something. He articulated what was wrong, and he stated clearly that it was your responsibility to fix it. If he told you to get it done, he expected it to get done. And if it wasn't done, you were in trouble and he spoke to you about it.

Finally, he was willing to do whatever was necessary to make things better, even if it caused people not to like him. There were times when he blew his top. There were also times when he fired people. But he was always respected because he was doing what was best for kids.

He was honest if he didn't like something. He held people accountable. And he cared about kids. That's why he was able to make a one-minute phone call to fix a major problem.

Chapter 49

Do Not Let the Obstacle Overcome You

It was a Thursday in October, about 6:30 p.m. The principal was working in his office doing paperwork and e-mails.

The phone rang and the principal picked it up. "May I help you?" the principal asked.

It was another principal. "This paperwork . . . these parents . . . these kids . . . these teachers . . . this job . . . the district office . . . my boss . . . I wish I were back in the classroom . . ."

* * *

Everybody has problems. And everybody gets down. And sometimes you need to vent and talk about your problems with other people.

But is it happening all the time with you? If you are frequently complaining about your problems to others, it can become a mindset where you are frequently complaining to yourself. Soon, it can become self-pity.

Instead of thinking of yourself as a strong leader who will find a way to solve the problems, you start thinking of yourself as a victim. You become what you think about. And you cannot be a strong leader if you are thinking of yourself as a victim.

When things get tough, you have to get yourself moving and focus on the solutions. Get out a piece of paper and start brainstorming about how to make things better. Then pick out the best ideas and start moving. Step-by-step, you can fix anything if you identify the problems, focus on the solutions, and move forward.

But you might not fix it the first time. So if plan A doesn't work, make up your mind ahead of time that you will come up with plan B. And if plan B doesn't work, come up with plan C.

Make up your mind that you will be mentally strong and never give up. Do not let the obstacle overcome you. Make up your mind that you will overcome the obstacle.

Chapter 50

Exhaustion

It was 4:30 p.m. The principal was sitting in his office with a ton of work to do. But he was so sleepy. He put his head down on the desk to rest his eyes for a few minutes.

When the principal woke up it was 5:30 p.m. He started working again. But the work went very slow. He was trying to write a simple memo, but he just couldn't get the words right. When he left to go home, it was 10:00 p.m.

As the principal drove home, he couldn't stop thinking about all of the work he had to do. And when he got home all he could think of was how tired he was. He was on a treadmill leading to exhaustion. And he didn't know how to get out of it.

The principal ate dinner and sat on the couch. He was asleep within five minutes.

* * *

You cannot be a powerful leader if you are worn out and exhausted. You cannot be skilled in working with people if you are tired and cranky. You cannot have an optimistic outlook if you are constantly fatigued. You cannot exercise good judgment if you are not thinking clearly.

It is also important to remember that a big part of leadership is setting a positive example. You are not setting a positive example for others if you are constantly exhausted. Instead, you are encouraging them to become sleep deprived themselves.

The long-term effects of sleep deprivation are no joke. It will cause permanent damage to your brain. It will ruin your physical health. And it will impair your ability to lead.

You are in denial if you think you can deprive yourself of sleep and be an effective leader. You cannot be at your best if you are exhausted. The only way to conquer exhaustion is to face reality and make sure that you get enough sleep.

Chapter 51

A Mistake He Would Never Forget

Lunch was over. The principal started walking with the students toward the classrooms by the girl's gym.

One minute before the tardy bell rang, the area was almost clear. The principal called out a warning, "You have one minute!" he said. "Let's go! Get inside your classroom!"

With thirty seconds left before the tardy bell, the principal called out again, "Thirty seconds!" he said. "Let's go, go, go! I want you inside your classroom!"

The tardy bell rang and the principal saw three students running toward their classrooms. They were about forty yards away.

"Gentlemen!" the principal called out. "Come here please!"

The students acted like they didn't hear the principal and continued running.

"Gentlemen!" yelled the principal as loud as he could. "Turn around and come back this way!"

But the students kept running and entered their classroom.

When the principal got to the students' classroom, the door was still open. The principal was upset. The students were supposed to have gone to the guidance room for being late. The teacher, by allowing the students to enter late, had undermined the school's tardy policy.

The principal was mad at the students for running away. He was also mad at the teacher for letting the students enter the classroom late.

When the principal looked into the classroom where the students had run, he saw that all of the students were quiet and working. The teacher was at the front of the room getting something ready at his desk. It looked like it was going to be a good lesson.

Instead of talking to the teacher privately and in a professional manner, the principal spoke to the teacher in front of his entire class.

"Please remember that you are required to stand at your doorway and close your door when the tardy bell rings," said the principal to the teacher. "It is a school policy. Please don't let it happen again."

The principal felt terrible as he walked back to his office. It was a public reprimand and every student had heard him. He had embarrassed the teacher. He had also made himself look like an idiot. It was a mistake he would never forget.

* * *

You will not inspire people to do their best by losing your temper and giving public reprimands. It makes people feel terrible. It causes them to fear and hate you. And it is wrong.

What you as the leader give to others is what they will often pass on. If you as the leader give out negatives, those who are under you will also give out negatives. That's how you create a negative mindset in an organization. And that's how you create a toxic working and learning environment that is bad for everybody.

You cannot lead unless you have very good communication with people. And if you blow up and lose your temper, both you and the other person are going to be hesitant about communicating again.

People will lose faith in you as a leader if you become known for flying off the handle and losing your temper. People want leaders whom they can believe in. They want leaders who are smart and level-headed, with good judgment.

Every time you act wisely as a leader and make good decisions, you are increasing the faith that people have in you. But the more you demonstrate otherwise, the more they will lose faith in you.

The leaders who get the best results are those who inspire others. You will not inspire others by losing your temper and flying off the handle. You will inspire others by showing quiet wisdom and being considerate of others.

Chapter 52

Advice from a Pro

It was 5:30 p.m., the second week of September. The principal parked his car and entered the front door of the district office. He had just finished his first week as a new principal. He was now going to meet with the assistant superintendent for educational services.

"I want to let you know about a situation with one of your parents," said the assistant superintendent. "She has been vocal about issues at your school, and she did a lot of things to undermine the previous principal. She has gained a following among some of the parents and teachers, and they are listening to her."

"What should I do?" the principal asked.

"As soon as you can next week, give the parent a call and ask her to meet with you," said the assistant superintendent. "Be patient and listen to what she has to say. But don't make any promises. Whenever you have to make a major decision this year, be sure to have a public forum ahead of time where the parents can express their views. You should also listen to teachers and students. When you announce your decision, make sure that you can explain all of the reasons behind it."

"Anything else?" the principal asked.

"She may decide to attack you personally when she realizes that you are not going to comply with her wishes," said the assistant superintendent. "You will not win by trying to fight her. But sooner or later she will expose herself. People will see her motives and stop listening to her. Gradually, she will lose her following."

"Thanks," said the principal. "I will do that."

"How is everything else going?" the assistant superintendent asked.

"I feel pretty good," said the principal. "I am tired. But it's a happy tired."

"Can I give you some advice?" the assistant superintendent asked.

"Yes, definitely," said the principal.

"In every position I have held, there have been times when I have been highly challenged," said the assistant superintendent. "There is a Japanese saying about mental toughness, and I want you to remember it. The saying is this: Fall down seven times, stand up eight times."

"You are going to fall down," said the assistant superintendent. "It happens to everybody, so prepare for it now. When you fall down, no matter what, make up your mind that you will find a way to stand up."

* * *

When you become a principal, you have to find a way to work with everybody. Some people can become very vocal and extremely challenging. They can hurt your school, and they can hurt you. You have to find a way to neutralize them.

Keep thinking about the big picture, and keep thinking about your long-term image as a principal. The big picture is that you want your school to improve and your students to learn at high levels. You also want parents, students, and teachers to believe in you.

If you get into a conflict, do your best to be patient and wait for the other person to become exposed. Stay above the fight. Be dignified, be honest, and display good leadership.

And remember about the power of persistence and bouncing back from adversity. When you get knocked down, remember that it happens to everybody. And no matter how bad it gets, make up your mind that you will stand up.

Chapter 53

Target Practice

It was a lonely feeling. The principal had made a decision to change distribution procedures for class schedules on the first day of school. With 3,500 students, it was not an easy decision.

If the new procedures worked, class schedules would be issued efficiently and the school would have a smooth opening. If the new procedures did not work, the principal would be blamed for making a bad decision.

* * *

Picture a shooting gallery with lots of people shooting guns, and just one target. Guess what? As the principal, you are often the target. No matter what you do, people are going to take shots at you. So be ready and do everything possible not to get hit.

First, always be courteous to people. Listen carefully and never interrupt. Always be considerate. People rarely forget if somebody has been rude to them. The person whom you disrespect today could be the person who tries to bring you down tomorrow.

Next, think about your decisions carefully. Try to think of everything that could possibly go wrong and come up with a plan that avoids those problems. The more you think, the better it will go. The less you think, the more problems you will have.

When you do make a decision, it has to stick. You will not gain the confidence of people by constantly changing your mind.

Finally, you must never do anything to compromise your integrity. You cannot lead people if they do not believe in you. Just a few words that are not true can ruin your credibility and destroy your ability to lead.

Chapter 54

Ask for Advice

It was 3:30 p.m. when the principal returned to his office from dismissal. He was tired, frustrated, and worried. It was a serious problem. He wasn't sure what to do. He picked up the phone to call another principal. He also called his supervisor. He needed to get some advice.

* * *

Nobody has all of the answers. And nobody is perfect. But as a principal, you have a very bright spotlight on you. You have to do everything you can to not make a mistake.

Whenever you make a mistake it will be a setback to your students and your school. It will also damage your credibility and your ability to lead. Every time you do the right thing, it will help you. Every time you do the wrong thing, it will hurt you.

Do your best to learn from others. The more you ask for advice, the more success you will have. The less you ask for advice, the less success you will have.

Chapter 55

A Big Difference

It was Thursday at 5:00 p.m. The Rotary Club was having a barbecue for the faculty. They did this every year before back-to-school night to show appreciation to the teachers. After the barbecue, teachers would go to their classrooms to see parents.

The principal got his food and sat down with a group of teachers from the math department. He enjoyed having a conversation with teachers that was not about school.

* * *

Teachers are isolated in their classrooms all day long with kids. They often feel alone in their efforts to help kids learn. Many of them stay in their classrooms during lunch to provide extra help to kids. This is very hard work. And teachers often feel they are not appreciated.

Whenever you have a faculty activity and you do not have a reason to sit with the administrators, it is important that you sit with the teachers. This will get you closer to them. It also makes a statement that you care about teachers and appreciate their efforts. It is a little thing that can make a big difference.

Chapter 56

Always Watching You

It was Monday. The principal was meeting with the assistant principals. Each of the assistant principals had all been at the school for three years or more. The principal had been at the school for only eight days. On the previous Friday, the assistant principals had all dressed casually. Casual Fridays had been the norm at the school.

"The next thing I want to say is very important," said the principal. "I need you to dress on Fridays in the same way that you dress on the other days."

The assistant principals were silent.

"The reason why, is because the way you dress sends a message," said the principal. "It does not give a good impression to parents or teachers if you are dressed casual. It also sends a message that Friday is a day to take things easy.

We have to do our best and go forward every single day," said the principal. "I do not want anybody to get the idea that we have a casual attitude about improving this school. We must communicate that we are trying to improve every day, not just on some days."

* * *

One of your most important tasks as a leader is to inspire excellence. You cannot inspire excellence by modeling mediocrity. The people at your school must know that you are always working hard and that you are very serious about making your school better. They must know that you are pushing forward every day, not just some days, to bring about improvements. You communicate this attitude through your words. You also communicate it through your actions.

When you examine the lives of people who are champions, you learn that they do everything within their power to perform at the highest levels. They don't just do some of the things that are necessary to achieve success. They do everything.

It is the same with the way you dress. If you dress casually, it says that you have a casual attitude about your job. If you dress professionally, it says that you take your job seriously. You will not communicate excellence by dressing down. You will communicate excellence by dressing in a professional manner every day.

Chapter 57

Section Review

Your effectiveness as a leader will determine the success of your school. What are the most important elements in effective leadership?

1. Choose the direction for your school based upon valid research. Know the difference between research-based strategies and opinion-based strategies.
2. Understand that others are watching you. Demonstrate professionalism and be a positive role for students and teachers.
3. Delegate thoughtfully and have a system to monitor the tasks you assign.
4. Do not face problems alone. Ask for advice from colleagues and your supervisor.

PEOPLE

Chapter 58

In the Middle of Kids

It was 7:30 a.m. The principal could see from his window that a lot of students were now on the campus. He walked out of his door to the quad and started walking among the students. There were generally the same groups of kids in the same locations. He started walking all over the place, going to all of the groups.

Kids would come up to the principal and say hi. He would ask them how they were doing in their classes. They were playing around and laughing, just being kids. The principal could tell from their actions that they felt safe and secure. This was one of his major goals, for the campus to be calm and peaceful.

* * *

You will not achieve a peaceful campus and close relationships with students by staying in your office and doing paperwork. You will achieve it by walking throughout your campus, by observing in classrooms, and by making direct contact with kids.

Students need adults they can believe in and who are with them. Actions always speak louder than words, and your constant presence on the campus and in classrooms will tell students that you care about their welfare.

You must be there to help supervise your campus. This means before school, nutrition, lunch, and passing periods. You must also participate in supervision after school. It is reassuring to parents, because they see that you are actively supervising to ensure safety. It will also bring you closer to your students.

You will also gain direct contact with students by going into classrooms. You can tell kids that learning is important. But you are not demonstrating it unless you go into classrooms to see what they are really doing. And kids love it when you go into classrooms to see them learn.

The more contact you make with students, the more effective you will be as their principal and their leader.

Chapter 59

It Was Distorted and Very Negative

She was a reporter from a local newspaper. The principal had invited her to the school because he hoped she would write a positive story about their improvements. The principal was proud of the school. He sat with the reporter for a long time and spoke with her about the improvements at the school that were raising student achievement.

The principal showed data to the reporter illustrating that student achievement had improved significantly. He took her all around the campus, and they visited many classrooms. Everything she saw was positive. The reporter also observed an awards ceremony recognizing students who had improved and demonstrated outstanding citizenship.

As they walked around the campus, the principal noticed that the reporter gave her business card to many of the people she met. The reporter asked people to call her if they had any ideas for news stories.

Nothing was printed in the newspaper about the improvements. But two weeks later, there was a major story and a picture on the front page about a near fight. The article was true. But the picture and headline were distorted and very negative. The picture and headline gave the impression that the near fight had been a major incident. In reality, the school had responded effectively and done an excellent job to prevent a major incident.

* * *

Newspaper reporters are assigned by their editors to find stories and write the news. When you open a newspaper, you will see that most of the stories are about problems. How many of them are about positive events? Very few. It's the same way with school news.

If you are considering calling a reporter to do a positive story on your school, remember that it can backfire. Once you get one story published, there are probably going to be others. And because of the way in which newspapers work, most of the additional stories will be about problems.

Publicity does not teach kids. There is very little that a newspaper story can do to help your school. The news that really counts is the news that students bring home and tell their parents. If students are giving positive news to their parents, that's the news you want.

Chapter 60

People Need Time

It was twelve years before he would become a principal. He was teaching English at a junior high school. During periods one through four, he was in the classroom. During periods five and six, he served as a mentor teacher.

On Tuesday during period two, the mentor teacher received a phone message to call his supervisor at the district office.

"There is a teacher at another school," said the supervisor. "She just started last week, and she is off to a very rough start. She made a statement to the assistant principal that she was ready to quit. She has a period six conference. Maybe you can see her today and talk to her."

The mentor teacher drove to the new teacher's school immediately after period four. He felt a strong sense of urgency because he had also experienced a terrible start when he began teaching. He also had to hurry, because he had to be back at his own school for a meeting by 3:00 p.m.

It was the middle of period five when the mentor teacher entered the classroom of the new teacher. The new teacher was at the chalkboard explaining instructions for a writing assignment. It was a seventh-grade English class.

Only about half of the students were listening to the new teacher. The rest of them were fiddling around or talking. Two of the students were out of their seats walking around. The new teacher appeared to be frustrated.

Twenty minutes later the bell rang. The students left the classroom. The mentor teacher had about ten minutes to talk to the new teacher.

"Nice to meet you," said the mentor teacher. "I was asked to come and visit you by the district office."

"It has been hard this week," said the new teacher. "But I think everything will be okay if the students just start bringing their pencils."

In light of the serious problems he had observed, it surprised the mentor teacher that the new teacher had brought up such a minor issue.

"Why don't you just lend pencils to the students?" the mentor teacher asked.

"I don't think I should do that," said the new teacher. "That should be their job, to bring their own pencils"

"I don't see what the big deal is," said the mentor teacher. "The problem will be solved if you just lend pencils to the students."

"I don't think you are helping me," said the new teacher. She started to cry. Then she jumped up and rushed out of the classroom.

Instead of helping the new teacher, the mentor teacher had alienated her and made her cry. Why had that happened?

First, the mentor teacher had been in a hurry. He only had about ten minutes to talk with the new teacher because he had to be back at his own school by 3:00 p.m. Instead of taking the necessary time to develop a relationship, he tried to rush things.

Next, the new teacher was upset because things had not been going well. It is a terrible feeling when you cannot control students. The new teacher had been experiencing that frustration for seven days. Making suggestions to people when they are upset will often just make them more upset.

The mentor teacher should have slowed down with the new teacher and just listened to her. He also should have backed off on the pencil issue. He would have accomplished much more if he had simply introduced himself to the new teacher, listened, and scheduled a classroom observation and feedback for another time.

* * *

People are not machines. You have to listen to them, take time with them, and develop relationships with them before they will be ready to accept suggestions from you. People need time. Sometimes you have to go slow to go fast. Every time you try to rush the improvement process without being sensitive to people, you run the risk of alienating them and causing the improvement process to take longer.

Chapter 61

Suggestion or Requirement?

It was 11:15 a.m. The passing period had just ended, and the students were now in class. The principal and his supervisor were meeting together in the principal's office.
  "I think it would be a good idea if you . . ." said the supervisor.
  "Is that a suggestion, or a requirement?" the principal asked.
  "It is something that you really need to do," said the supervisor.
  "Okay," said the principal. "I will do it."

* * *

As a principal, it is necessary for you to show initiative and make decisions about what is best for your school. You cannot be an effective leader unless you take responsibility and have a take-charge attitude.

But you do not have the authority to do anything you want. And the relationship that you maintain with your supervisor is critical in making sure that you do not get yourself in trouble.

It is your responsibility to understand what your supervisor wants from you. Different supervisors have different styles. Some supervisors are direct, and they make it clear if you are required to do something. Some supervisors are indirect, and it is not always easy to know what they want.

Many supervisors are comfortable with principals who take a great deal of initiative to solve problems on their own. But many supervisors are not. If you are not clear about what is needed when you are speaking with your supervisor, it is very important that you ask.

Do not try to guess. Just ask.

Unless you are at the very top, it is a fact of life in any organization that you must be a team player. If you gain a reputation as a maverick, it can eventually spell the end of your career.

Know your supervisor and what he or she wants from you. Know the difference between suggestions and requirements. Do not jeopardize your career by failing to understand your boss.

Chapter 62

Saved by a Recording Device

It was a Thursday afternoon during the third week of March. It was 5:30 p.m. and the principal was sitting at his desk doing paperwork. It had been a busy week. On Tuesday and Wednesday they had given the California High School Exit Exam to all tenth graders.

An official from the teacher's union appeared at the principal's door. "Do you have a minute?" the official asked.

A probationary teacher who had received a non reelection notice was standing next to the union official. The non reelection notice meant that the probationary teacher would be released without cause at the end of the school year.

The union official had not made an appointment to see the principal. He had probably shown up at 5:30 p.m. to catch the principal alone and off guard.

"Come in," said the principal. "Have a seat."

The two men entered the office and sat down.

The union official began speaking. "Do you think it is fair the way these non reelections are being handled?" the official asked. "Do you think it is right to dismiss a highly qualified teacher who is doing an excellent job?"

The union official was trying to bait the principal and get him to provide a reason why the teacher's probationary contract was not being renewed. The teacher had consistently performed below standard. The principal and an assistant principal had observed the teacher several times and met with him to discuss improvements that were needed. Unfortunately, the teacher had not improved. Non reelection notices are issued without cause. If the principal explained the reason for the non reelection, the union would have grounds to appeal.

"As you know," said the principal, "It was a non reelection without cause. I am not at liberty to discuss anything about a non reelection."

"Why is that?" the union official asked. "Can't you talk about the reasons why you do things?"

"I am not going to discuss anything about a non reelection," said the principal.

"Is that the right way to treat teachers?" the official asked. "Don't teachers deserve an explanation for what is happening to them?"

The principal pulled out his cell phone and activated the sound recorder.

"This conversation is now being recorded," said the principal.

Nothing more was said. The union official and the teacher both left the office.

* * *

Using a recording device is a smart way to deal with situations where you need a witness. It will assist you in handling conversations where the other person is becoming unreasonable. It will also protect you from being accused of something that you did not say.

Chapter 63

Necessary Action

When the principal returned to his office, he found a sealed envelope on his desk. The envelope contained a complaint by a parent who had telephoned him the day before. According to the parent, a science teacher had made humiliating remarks to her daughter.

The principal had earlier asked the parent to make a written statement so that he could investigate and take necessary action. The accused teacher was a veteran who had been displaced from another high school.

On the following morning, the principal met with the assistant principal who was over the science department.

"I need you to investigate a complaint that I received from a parent," said the principal.

"What happened?" the assistant principal asked.

"The parent states that the teacher called her daughter a 'stupid idiot,' a 'dummy,' and a 'child of the devil.'"

"That's terrible," said the assistant principal.

"I need you to investigate this fully," said the principal. "First, I need you to interview the daughter and get a written statement. Make sure the statement is detailed about what the teacher said."

"Okay," said the assistant principal.

"After that, I need you to interview at least five randomly selected students from that class to find out what they heard," said the principal. "When you meet with the students, do not share the allegations that were made. Just tell them you are doing an investigation and ask if they are aware of any staff members in the school who have made inappropriate comments to students."

"Follow up and interview additional witnesses based upon what the randomly selected students tell you," said the principal. "I am going to call the

principal of the previous school to find out if there were any similar problems in the past."

"How soon do you need this done?" the assistant principal asked.

"Please do your best to complete the interviews today," said the principal. "These are serious allegations. I want to get this resolved right away."

* * *

Allegations of employee misconduct must be addressed quickly and thoroughly. If the allegations are true and you do not respond properly, the misconduct will likely happen again. You also risk having others gain the belief that you are afraid to deal with misconduct, or that you condone it. This would seriously jeopardize your ability to lead.

First, you or another administrator should talk to witnesses and obtain written statements. These statements should be handwritten in ink to make it clear they are the actual words of the witnesses. If the allegations are about inappropriate language that was used, be sure the statements include the exact words spoken, including any profanity.

If a problem is relatively minor and has not happened before, it is appropriate to handle the problem informally. This could involve having an assistant principal meet with the employee and keep an informal record of the meeting.

If the allegations are serious or if similar allegations have occurred previously, you need to conduct a formal conference. The employee should be allowed to bring a representative to the meeting. A second administrator should also attend as a witness. Documentation should include a conference summary which is placed in the employee's personnel file.

It is very important that you draft the conference summary ahead of time. It should include everything you intend to say. During the conference, you should read from the draft to ensure you do not get sidetracked. Be sure to include a clear directive which tells the employee not to engage in the misconduct again. This makes it possible to proceed with higher levels of discipline if there is a further problem.

Chapter 64

It Was Said Behind His Back

It was about 8:30 a.m. on a Friday in November. The principal was getting ready to go into a classroom when he got a radio call to come to the office.

It was a phone call from a district administrator. "I had an interesting conversation with two of your union representatives," said the administrator.

"What happened?" the principal asked.

"Yesterday afternoon I met with all of the union reps," said the administrator. "After the meeting, the two reps from your school asked to speak with me confidentially. I thought it was going to be something bad. Instead, they thanked me for hiring you. They talked about how hard you worked, and about how the school had improved so much."

"Wow!" said the principal.

"I have been doing this for a long time," said the administrator. "During all my years, I have never had union representatives come up and give such praise to a principal."

* * *

It doesn't matter very much what people say to your face. What matters is what they think. And what matters is what they say behind your back. If you are working hard and doing your best, people are going to notice. They will appreciate your efforts, even if they don't say it to your face.

The same thing goes for listening and showing respect for people. When you really listen to other people, when you look at them when they are talking to you, and when you never interrupt them, you are showing respect and consideration for what they are saying. They might not agree with every decision that you make. But they will respect you for listening to them.

You must work hard to help your school improve. You must also make it a very high priority to have good relationships with your union representatives. You should go to their classrooms and keep them informed whenever there is a major problem or event taking place at the school. And when they come to you with a problem, you should listen to them very carefully and do your best to solve the problem.

You will not always agree. But you must always listen and show respect. The positive relationship that you build will pay off in helping your school improve.

Chapter 65

It Was a Lie and the Principal Believed Him

The interview committee consisted of the social studies chair, two additional social studies teachers, an assistant principal, and the principal. When the final interview was completed, the committee discussed all four of the candidates.

They finished talking after about 20 minutes. The principal gave each of the committee members a card to rate the candidates. The final candidate was rated the highest. He had requested a transfer from a middle school to a high school.

On the following day, the principal called the final candidate's middle school to get a reference. The principal of the middle school gave a glowing recommendation. He said that the candidate was outstanding.

They hired the teacher.

On the third day of school, the principal went into the teacher's classroom to observe him. About half of the students were socializing. The rest of the students were doing a worksheet that appeared to be busywork. The bulletin boards were empty, and nothing had been done to fix up the classroom. When the principal asked to look at the teacher's lesson plan, the teacher pointed to the agenda on the whiteboard.

It was not what the principal had expected to see. The previous principal had lied to him.

* * *

It is wrong to give a good recommendation to get rid of a bad teacher. If you have a bad teacher, do your job and give a below-standard evaluation. Don't cause another school to suffer because you did not want to do your job.

Chapter 66

Gossip

It was 8:15 a.m. at the school district office. The meeting was scheduled to begin in fifteen minutes. The principal sat down and turned on his laptop to take notes. A program coordinator came over and sat next to him. The principal had known the program coordinator for several years.

The program coordinator had a lot to say: "The parents have been complaining at.... There was a big problem at.... The instructional coach at..."

The principal did not want to listen to this. "I am going to get a cup of coffee," he said. "I will be right back."

* * *

People are always going to gossip. It can help your career if the gossip is positive. But it can destroy your career if the gossip is negative. So what should you do about it?

First, do your best to make sure that any gossip about you is positive. This means always doing your best, always working hard, and always being professional.

Next, do your best to prevent others from wanting to say anything bad about you. This means always treating others with respect and courtesy. It also means doing your best to be helpful to others.

Make sure that you never spread gossip yourself. As a leader, it is important that you hold yourself to a higher standard. Participating in gossip is wrong. It also makes you look bad. You will undermine your career if you participate in gossip, because others will lose faith in you.

Chapter 67

Delay Makes It Worse

It was a Tuesday morning during the third week of December. The principal had asked the teacher to meet with him at 9:00 a.m. He had been putting off meeting with the teacher because he felt bad about what he was going to say.

"I appreciate the effort you have made during the last two months," said the principal. "I know that you have tried very hard."

A worried look came over the teacher's face.

"I have visited your classroom and met with you to provide feedback," said the principal. "The instructional coach has also been working with you. But the situation has not improved."

The teacher looked down. She knew what was coming next.

"Your contract expires on December 30," said the principal. "I need to let you know that it will not be extended past that date. Your last day of employment here will be this Friday."

"I know that I have been struggling," said the teacher. "And I don't have any hard feelings. I just wish you had told me earlier. That way I would have had more time to plan what to do next."

* * *

It is always difficult to give bad news. But if you procrastinate, you will often make it worse. No matter how bad it is, be fair to the recipient and give the bad news as quickly as you can.

Chapter 68

Talk to the Person in Person

It was 10:15 a.m. The principal was out on the school grounds when he received a radio message that he had an important telephone call.

When the principal reached his office, the secretary told him that the superintendent was on the line. The principal picked up the telephone.

"I need to talk to you," said the superintendent. "Do you think you could come over here?"

"Do you want me to come now?" said the principal.

"Yes, please come now," said the superintendent.

The principal drove to the school district office. It was three miles away. He had no idea what the superintendent wanted to discuss with him. The principal did not like being off campus during school time. He hoped there was not a problem.

When the principal reached the superintendent's office, the secretary said that he could go right in.

"Thanks for getting here so quickly," said the superintendent. "I have a question that I wanted to ask . . ."

Five minutes later, the meeting was over.

As the principal was driving back to his school, it seemed strange to him that the superintendent had not just asked him the question over the phone. Then he realized why the superintendent had wanted to speak with him in person.

A school board member had called the superintendent with a concern that had been raised by a parent. It was a very serious concern. The superintendent needed to know the absolute truth.

When the superintendent asked the question, he was looking at the principal's face. The superintendent knew by the principal's facial expressions and his eyes that he was telling the truth. A phone call would not have told him that.

* * *

You need all the help you can get when you are communicating with other people. You need to understand them, and they need to understand you. How do you create the best understanding possible when you are communicating with others?

First, try as much as you can to communicate in person. Listen to the other person carefully, and look at the other person's facial expressions and eyes. When you communicate in person, you get the benefit of the nonverbal cues that people use when they are talking with each other. You can ask questions. It is also easier to tell if the other person is being honest with you.

If you cannot communicate in person, the next best way is to make a telephone call. You cannot get the visual clues that you can get by talking in person. But you can certainly give and get clues via tone of voice. You also get the benefit of being able to ask questions.

When it comes to communicating via e-mail, be sure to remember the pitfalls. Communicating accurately in writing can be difficult, and it is very easy to write something that can cause a misunderstanding. It is very difficult to judge the truthfulness of an e-mail. And with e-mail there is no privacy. Anything you write can easily be forwarded to everybody in your school district.

Whenever you get an e-mail that involves something which needs to discussed, it is a good idea to telephone the person or send a reply asking the other person to call you. From there, you can set up a face-to-face meeting. It might take more time in the short run. But in the long run, talking in person can prevent misunderstandings and save a great deal of time.

Chapter 69

You Must Also Be Persuasive

It was 5:30 p.m. when the principal left the district office. He had met with his supervisor regarding a proposal to improve student achievement. The supervisor had failed to approve the proposal. The principal was so frustrated.

As he was driving back to his school, the principal thought about the meeting and started reflecting on what he could have done better:

1. *Was it a strong proposal that would improve student achievement? Yes.*
2. *Had the proposal been successful at other schools? Yes.*
3. *Had the principal looked at the research? Yes.*
4. *Had the principal spoken to people at his school to get their ideas? Yes.*
5. *Had the principal made a careful plan of what he would present to his supervisor? No.*

The principal failed because he had not made a careful plan of how he would present the proposal. Careful planning would have made all the difference.

* * *

It is not enough just to have a proposal that you think is good. You must also be able to convince others. How do you convince others to believe in your ideas?

First, you must understand the available research behind your proposal. You must also know about the experiences of others who have implemented the proposal. You should avoid presenting a proposal that has not been tested elsewhere.

Next, you should talk to others at your school and get their ideas. This means speaking with students, teachers, parents, and other administrators.

The next step is to develop a plan that will encompass all of the information you have received. Keep working until you know the idea will work. Try to think of all possible objections, and fully address those objections.

Finally, you need to make your plan presentable. You must be able to clearly explain how your plan will address the need. You must also be able to outline the next steps needed to implement the plan.

If the principal had followed these steps before speaking with his supervisor, he probably would have been able to sell the proposal. A few minutes of additional thought and planning would have made all the difference.

Chapter 70

Remember the Positives

It was a Friday at 11:30 p.m. The principal parked his car on the street and walked across the grass to the front steps. He thought about the class where he had seen bad teaching that day. He thought about the near fight after the football game. He thought about the school-improvement report that was now overdue to the district office.

It was nice to be home. It had been a tough day.

But then he thought about the positives. He had observed some great classrooms where the students had been learning at high levels. During lunch, the students had loved it when the band had marched around the campus playing the music they would play at the football game. He had helped a student who needed information about college.

It was nice to be home. It had also been a successful day.

* * *

As a principal, you are often all alone. The weight of a school can be very heavy. And if things go wrong, the blame will fall on you.

When things go right, be sure to give yourself credit for helping to make your school better. Keep remembering your accomplishments and the efforts you are making every day to help students. Think about all of the things you do behind the scenes to support classroom instruction. And feel proud of yourself for the difference you are making in the lives of your students.

Chapter 71

A Good School Again

It was 4:30 p.m. on a Wednesday in June. The meeting was over, and everybody else had left. The principal was speaking with a department chair who had been at the school for almost forty years.

"This school was out of control for a long time," said the department chair. "You helped us become a good school again."

"Thanks," said the principal.

"What I noticed is that you didn't really do anything that special," said the department chair. "You just worked hard and made sure that things were done right."

* * *

The school had been out of control for many years. Truancy, fighting, gang activity, and racial conflicts had occurred regularly. Teachers doing their best under difficult conditions had not been getting the support they needed. Student achievement had been very low.

Finally, the school improved. It happened because of discipline policies that brought about improved student conduct. It happened because of administrators visiting classrooms and providing teachers with the support they needed. It happened because of efforts to build hope and recognize students for working hard.

Most of the changes were implemented during the first two years. But the results took time. By the third year, people began to believe that the improvements were real. By the fifth year, people began to believe that it was a good school again.

The improvements have continued. Test scores have risen steadily. More students are going to college every year. And there is a great sense of pride. What a wonderful success for everybody!

Chapter 72

Section Review

As a principal, you are working all day with people. The more effective you are in working with others, the more you will improve student achievement. Remember the following when you are working with the people at your school:

1. Listen carefully to others, make eye contact when they are speaking with you, and never interrupt. Listen, listen, listen.
2. Stay close to your students. Get into classrooms and interact with them. Move about among students during passing periods, lunch, and after school. Speak with them and really get to know them.
3. Stay close to your staff. Talk with teachers every day and value their ideas about improving student achievement. Look for ways to interact with teachers informally. Make sure they know you are supporting them.
4. Stay close to your supervisor. Discuss ideas for improving student achievement. Make sure you understand the difference between suggestions and requirements.
5. Remember the positives. Give yourself credit every day for the efforts you are making to help students learn at the highest levels and achieve their dreams.

Index

administrator, 5, 7–8, 29, 39, 44–45, 55, 71–72, 95, 103, 116, 119, 121–22, 149, 168–69, 179, 183
adversity, 144
advice, 16, 130, 147, 153
alumni, 69
announcement, 96
assistant superintendent, 101, 143–44
award, 31–32, 159

beach, 93–94
block scheduling, 55
boss, 137, 164

casual Friday, 151
checking for understanding, 43, 63, 84–85
classroom, xvi–xvii, 3–5, 8, 11–13, 15–17, 26, 29, 36, 41, 43–45, 47–49, 51–53, 55–61, 65–67, 71, 83–85, 89, 93, 107, 119, 122, 129–30, 137, 141, 149, 157–59, 161–62, 169–71, 175, 181, 183, 185
classroom observation, 51, 53, 66, 162
class rules, 16
class schedules, 91, 93, 96, 100, 145
class sizes, 91, 99–100
Common Core State Standards, 71–82
communication, 23, 105–6, 114, 131, 142
complaint, 59–60, 101, 120–21, 167

contract, 58, 103–4, 107, 128, 165, 175
crisis, 95–97

deadline, 90, 111, 113, 115–16
deceased student, 96–97
decision, 120, 127–28
delay, 175
delegation, 92, 111–13, 115, 153
department chair, 48, 117, 123–24, 183
detention, 8, 11–13, 17, 19, 29–30
discipline (employee), 114, 120, 168
discipline (student), 3–4, 7, 12, 16, 26, 39, 57, 61, 96, 121, 130, 183
drown, 93, 112, 124

earthquake drill, 33
e-mail, 137, 178
exhaustion, 129, 139–40

fall down, 144
fight, 3, 5, 7, 15, 24–27, 30, 33–37, 119–21, 143–44, 159, 181, 183
firework, 59
first day, 61, 89, 93, 129, 131, 145

gang, xv, 5, 7–8, 23–24, 26, 35–37, 57, 95–97, 107, 119, 130–31, 183
gossip, 119, 173
graffiti, 57, 89–90, 97
grief, 13, 95–96, 107

gunfire, 95–96

infraction, 12, 19
instructional coach, 4, 15, 57, 129–30, 173, 175

Japanese saying, 144

leadership, xvi, xix, 44, 66, 69, 90, 105, 112, 130–32, 135, 139, 144, 153
learning, xvii, 4, 7, 9, 16–17, 39, 43, 45, 48, 55–56, 60, 63–64, 66–67, 69–70, 84, 90, 99–100, 122, 128, 131, 142, 157, 181
learning environment, 4, 69–70, 142
learning standards, 43, 63, 84

management, 113–14
master schedule, 91–92, 99–100, 107, 120–21
maverick, 164
medal, 31–32
meeting, xvi, 7–8, 15, 37, 44–45, 48, 51, 53, 65, 71, 89, 101, 103–6, 117–18, 123, 125, 127, 129, 151, 161, 163, 168–69, 173, 175, 177–79, 183

newspaper, 159–60
new teacher, xvi, 15–16, 61–62, 129, 161–62
non re-election, 165–66

opinion-based, 63–64, 85, 153
Opportunity Academy, 117

parent meeting, 48
persistence, 144
persuasive, 73–74, 78, 80, 82, 179
phone call, 12, 17, 59, 67, 101, 135–36, 169, 177, 178
positive recognition, 17, 32, 39
procrastinate, 175
PTA, 65

quiet voices, 123–24

racial, 5, 7, 33, 35–37, 183
radio, 3, 23, 25–26, 33, 59, 95, 119, 169, 177
recording device, 165–66
relationships, 24, 48, 74–76, 79, 118–20, 157, 162–63, 170
reprimand, 142
research, 48, 56, 63–64, 73, 78, 80, 82, 85, 124, 130, 132, 153, 179
restroom, 58, 89, 97, 23
riot, 5, 35, 37
Rotary Club, 149

sacrifice, 119
Saturday school, 19–21
shooting gallery, 145
sleep, 57, 129, 139–40
small learning community, 7, 99–100
socializing, 51, 57, 120, 171
sod, 135
special program, 117
Sports Illustrated, 51–52
stand up, 93, 103, 144
supervision, 5, 11, 23, 25–26, 34, 36–37, 89, 96–97, 115, 157
suspension, 21, 26–27, 29–30
sustained silent reading, 47–49, 51–52, 123–24

teaching, xvi–xvii, 4, 9, 15–17, 39, 56, 60–61, 63, 66, 71, 85, 123, 129–32, 161, 181
telephone call, 12, 17, 59, 67, 101, 135–36, 169, 177, 178
test scores, 125, 184
TGIF, 119
tragedy, 93–96

union, 103–4, 165–66, 169–70, 187
urgency, 161

vandalism, 90
video, 36, 55

weeds, 89–90

About the Author

Russ Thompson, Ed.D., served as an educator for thirty-six years with the Los Angeles Unified School District and the Centinela Valley Union High School District. He served as a teacher, mentor teacher, and dean at Bret Harte and Gompers junior high schools. He served as a dean and assistant principal at Roosevelt, Locke, and Westchester high schools. He spent fourteen years as the principal of Van Nuys, Leuzinger, and Gardena high schools. He also served as a principal leader and director of high school services.

He earned a bachelor's degree in English and physical education from Whitworth College (now Whitworth University). He received a credential as a reading specialist and a master's degree in education from California State University, Dominguez Hills. He earned a doctorate in education from the University of California at Los Angeles.

www.ingramcontent.com/pod-product-compliance
Lightning Source LLC
Chambersburg PA
CBHW030138240426
43672CB00005B/172